I.A. Richards and New Criticism

I.A. Richards and New Criticism

Ashok Kumar

ATLANTIC
PUBLISHERS & DISTRIBUTORS (P) LTD

Published by

ATLANTIC

PUBLISHERS & DISTRIBUTORS (P) LTD

7/22, Ansari Road, Darya Ganj,
New Delhi-110002
Phones : +91-11-40775252, 23273880, 23275880, 23280451
Fax : +91-11-23285873
Web : www.atlanticbooks.com
E-mail : orders@atlanticbooks.com

Branch Office
5, Nallathambi Street, Wallajah Road,
Chennai-600002
Phones : +91-44-64611085, 32413319
E-mail : chennai@atlanticbooks.com

ISBN 978-81-269-1341-1

Printed in India at Nice Printing Press, A-33/3A, Site-IV, Industrial Area, Sahibabad, Ghaziabad, U.P.

Preface

Modern critics have endeavoured to discuss the nature and function of poetry. T.S. Eliot and I.A. Richards, whose influences combined to stimulate New Criticism, were particularly concerned with this problem. I.A. Richards has been one of the most influential of modern critics who have endeavoured to analyse the precise nature of poetry and to distinguish it from scientific discourse. His *Principles of Literary Criticism* came out in 1924. What we have been calling modern criticism began in 1924 with the publication of Richards's epoch-making book.

Though a scientist by training and habit, Richards was always a poet by nature and temperament. In his definition of a poem, Richards departs radically from the conception of poetry. According to him, poetry affords the clearest examples of the subordination of reference to attitude. It is the supreme form of the emotive use of language. The bulk of poetry consists of statements which are not verifiable. In *Science and Poetry* (1926), Richards coined a special phrase "pseudo-statement" to explain statements of the kind made in poetry. This term anticipates Carnap's "pseudo-object sentences," suggested some seven years later in *Logical Syntax of Language* (1933). Carnap considered most sentences to be formed sentences in material disguise. But, Richards is concerned with their truth or falsity.

As one of the seminal thinkers paving the way for the development of New Criticism, Richards made a systematic attempt to formulate a theory of poetry in consonance with the demands of modern scientific thought. Richards's writings had a powerful impact on nearly two generations of critics. In his crusade against speculative metaphysics and aesthetic thinking, derived from transcendental philosophy, Richards makes a determined attempt to replace traditional aesthetic philosophy by a strict scientific discipline, pragmatism and utilitarianism.

A general impression has been created that from *Coleridge On Imagination* (1934) onwards, through *The Philosophy of Rhetoric* (1936) and *Speculative Instruments*(1955) to *So Much Nearer* (1960), there is a radical shift in Richards's aesthetic thinking. It is alleged that in his early writings, Richards assigned an inferior status to poetry by calling it as a "pseudo-statement" in *Science and Poetry* (1926). However, the study of the later writings of Richards led me to refute the charges levelled against him. Richards has ever been a passionate lover of poetry and the emotive use of words. We have to realize that corresponding to the two uses of language, Richards has developed two angles of vision. He quotes Blake as saying "The eye, altering, alters all." Richards's early books had been designed in terms of the scientific or the camera eye. His later books show the alteration of his scientific eye in the "emotive eye." And so he comes to define poetry in Coleridgean terms as the completest mode of utterance. Like Coleridge, Richards sees poetry as bringing the whole soul of man into activity and at the same time imposing upon it a more than usual order, and like him, he teaches that to experience poetry fully is to enjoy the bliss of the rectified mind and the freed heart. Richards's thinking proceeds logically to its grand finale in his prophetic vision of poetry being an "unacknowledged legislation of the world." I humbly submit that there is an essential continuity between Richards's early and later writings and between Richards's theory of poetry and New Criticism.

I have tried to trace the subtle shifts in Richards's theory of poetry as we move to his later writings. I have also tried to trace the essential continuity of Richards's theory of poetry in New Criticism. Richards's conception of poetry in his later writings is tinctured by Coleridge's organic and integral view of poetry. Dr. Richards gave a new direction, a new dimension, to the criticism of poetry in an age dominated by science. According to Richards, no separation can be made between form and content, between message and signal in poetry. I have tried to lay threadbare the foundation of literary criticism propounded by I.A. Richards which paved the way for New Criticism which, in turn, helped in widening the scope of discipline of English studies. Though New Criticism has now branched out in several directions and critics have sounded a note of dissent against Richards, New Criticism seems to persist in seeking a place in our contemporary scheme of things and I.A. Richards remains a milestone in the history of criticism.

I wish to acknowledge my indebtedness to the writers of all those books and journals which have directly or indirectly contributed to this work. Last but not least, I acknowledge my indebtedness to Atlantic Publishers and Distributors (P) Ltd., New Delhi, for heartily undertaking the publication of this book.

Ashok Kumar

Contents

New Bearings in Modern Criticism

1

Criticism is a phase of literary expression as significant as the creative. In the words of T.S. Eliot, "each generation brings to the contemplation of art its own categories of appreciation, makes its own demand upon art and has its own uses for art."[1] Literary criticism will change as the world changes. Eliot rightly argues that every generation must provide its own literary criticism. Each generation looks at masterpieces of the past in a different perspective and it is affected in its attitude by a greater number of influences than those which bore upon generation previously. The intellectual and emotional climate of our time has something to do with the characteristic development of literary criticism in the present age.

An important work of literary criticism can alter and expand the context of the term "literary criticism" itself. The evolution of the term 'literary criticism' is interesting. Sidney's *Apology for Poetry* and Dryden's *An Essay of Dramatic Poesy* represent the early stage of literary criticism in England. Dryden has been described by Dr. Johnson as "the father of English criticism."[2] In the true sense of the term, criticism which discusses principles and determines merit, begins with Dryden. Johnson's *Lives of the Poets* is a critical masterpiece—"a masterpiece of the judicial bench."[3] Johnson represents the tradition of neo-classicism to the end of which he himself belongs. To Johnson, poetry is the art of uniting pleasure with truth. Johnson pays tribute to the verdict of readers. By the phrase "the common reader," Johnson meant the ordinary educated reader of poetry of his day. Johnson was a pure critic. He took literature as literature.

The nineteenth century was not one of the great ages of literary criticism, yet both the eighteenth and the nineteenth centuries have been called "the age of criticism" for the emergence of two critical masterpieces in the form of *Lives of the Poets* in the eighteenth century and *Biographia Literaria* in the nineteenth century. Arthur Symons has described *Biographia Literaria* as the greatest book of criticism in English.[4] Though Coleridge never completed his grand philosophical system, he did work out his theory of imagination and its implications for the art of poetry in considerable detail. For Coleridge, the primary imagination is the great ordering principle involved in acts of perception. The secondary imagination is more conscious and less elemental, but it does not differ in kind from primary imagination, it projects and creates new harmonies of meaning. The employment of secondary imagination is, in the larger sense, a poetic activity. "The poet, described in ideal perfection, brings the whole soul of man into activity."[5] A poem, in the narrower sense, is defined by Coleridge as "that species of composition, which is opposed to works of science, by proposing for its immediate object pleasure, not truth, and from all other species... it is discriminated by proposing to itself such delight from the whole, as is compatible with a distinct gratification from each component part." Coleridge points out that anything in rhyme and metre is a poem but a legitimate poem is one "the parts of which mutually support and explain each other; all in their proportion harmonizing with, and supporting the purpose and known influences of metrical arrangements."[6] To Coleridge's mind, poetry is essentially ideal and generic. Coleridge brought a wide scope and variety of interests to bear in his discussion of poetry. As T.S. Eliot points out, Coleridge "established the relevance of philosophy, aesthetics and psychology, and once Coleridge had introduced these disciplines into literary criticism, future critics could ignore them only at their own risk."[7] There is essentially something modern about Coleridge. A modern critic can find much in common with Coleridge. To quote Eliot once again, "The criticism of today indeed, may be said to be in direct descent from Coleridge, who would.... were he alive now, take the same interest in the social sciences and in the study of language and semantics, that he took in the sciences available to him."[8]

Matthew Arnold's *Essays in Criticism* is another important landmark in the history of criticism. If Ruskin took art as his guide to the deficiencies of contemporary civilization, Matthew Arnold took literature, and literature itself, as the type of culture. According to Arnold, poetry should deal not with ideas which are abstract, but with life; for life is action, dynamic and moving towards an end, to him, poetry is criticism of life. Poetry must deal with life and action in a spirit of high seriousness, of moral earnestness. In the age of Charles Darwin, T.H. Huxley and Tyndall, Arnold found the factual basis of religion threatened by modern knowledge and he sought to find in poetry a source of values which could not be threatened by the new scientific knowledge. The connection between his view of poetry and his view of literature can be seen in the opening paragraph of the essay "The Study of Poetry" which he contributed as an introduction towards English Poets (1980), "Our religion has materialized itself in the fact, in the supposed fact; it has attached its emotion to the fact, and now the fact is failing it. But for poetry the idea is everything; the rest is a world of illusion, of divine illusion. Poetry attaches its emotion to the idea; the idea is the fact. The strongest part of our religion today is its unconscious poetry."[9] So Arnold wrote in 1879/1880. Richards quoted Arnold's statement in 1926 in his *Science and Poetry*. Arnold was concerned in finding for poetry, or imaginative literature in general, a kind of meaning and a kind of usefulness which differentiated it clearly from science and freed it from any direct responsibility towards scientific truth. Richard too, was concerned with the same problem of finding a relevance for poetry in a world dominated by scientific materialism. The Arnoldian prophecy rings out in the opening paragraph of his essay, "The future of poetry is immense, because in poetry, where it is worthy of its high destinies, our race, as time goes on, will find an ever surer and surer stay".[10] This is an eloquent statement of the significance and value of poetry, but the nature and function of poetry has to be explained. Arnold goes on to say in a didactic prophetic vein: "More and more mankind will discover that we have to turn to poetry to interpret life for us, to console us, to sustain us. Without poetry, our science will appear incomplete, and most of what now passes with us for religion and philosophy will be replaced by poetry."[11] Hence, Arnold marks out a didactic function for poetry, but he does not have the optimism frenzy of Shelley who, in his *Defence of Poetry*, pictures the poet as inspired rhapsodist capturing in language the moments of his contact with the ideal world. From the Arnoldian point of view, we have a paramount responsibility to discover what is truly great poetry. Arnold goes on to say that "the best poetry is what we want; the best poetry will be found to have a power of forming, sustaining, and delighting us, as nothing else can".[12] Arnold appears to be more concerned with discovering the means of distinguishing the best poetry from inferior kinds than in describing in accurate detail what poetry, indeed, is and how it operates.

Modern critics have endeavoured to discuss the nature and function of poetry. T.S. Eliot and I.A. Richards, whose influences combined to stimulate New Criticism, were particularly concerned with this problem. I.A. Richards has been one of the most influential of modern critics who have endeavoured to analyse the precise nature of poetry and to distinguish it from scientific discourse. Richards, like the Russian formalists, dealt with literature directly stressing the need to focus our attention on the written text rather than on the paratextual areas like biographical and historical facts. He was merely interested in reader's response to literature. His criticism took the direction of aesthetic-psychological analysis. *Practical Criticism* records his experiments with his Cambridge students in which he distributed poems for analysis without giving any hint to the poet's name or biography. He just wanted each student to record his/her response to the text. The result convinced Richards of the need to evolve a system aiming at rigorous training in reading of poetry and he himself proposed a number of initial measures. He began with locating the strands of meaning that a poetic language contained. His *Principles of Literary Criticism* came out in 1924. What we have been calling modern criticism began in 1924, with the publication of Richards's epoch-making book. Criticism has developed and branched out in several directions. The new trends of criticism have no doubt, roots in the past, are not without antecedents and are not absolutely original. Still, René Wellek distinguishes in *Concepts of Criticism*, at least six general trends which are new in the twentieth century. He refers to the following major trends:

(1) Marxist criticism, (2) Psycho-analytic criticism, (3) Linguistic and Stylistic criticism, (4) A new Organistic formalism, (5) Myth criticism appealing to the results of cultural anthropology and the speculations of Carl Jung and (6) What amounts to a new Philosophical criticism inspired by existentialism and kindered world views.

I go on to comment briefly on the trends in modern criticism with particular reference to the conception of poetry embodied in such critical formulations of ideas. In taste and theory Marxist criticism grows out of the realistic criticism of the nineteenth century. It appeals to a few pronouncements made by Marx and Engels. Prescriptive Marxism asks the writer to reproduce reality accurately in the depiction of contemporary society. Stalin described writers as the engineers of the human soul,[13] while Marxist criticism, on the one hand, calls upon the writer to depict contemporary society with an insight into its structure, on the other hand, it asks the writer to be a socialist-realist. This, in practice, means that he is not to reproduce reality objectively but must use his art to spread socialism, i.e. communism; the party-spirit and the party-line. This criticism has become an organ of party-discipline not only in Russia and its many satellites, but apparently also in China. Even the genuine insights of Marxism into social processes and economic motivations are hardly used today. In England Christopher Caudwell (1907-37) was the outstanding Marxist critic. His main book *Illusion and Reality* (1937) is actually "a weird mixture of Marxian anthropology and psycho-analysis, a diatribe against individualistic civilization and false burgeois freedom."[14] Marxism is at its best when it serves as a device to expose the latent social and ideological implications of a work of literature.

The second of the six critical trends listed about psycho-analysis is based on the discoveries of Freud about the mind. Freud himself suggested the leading motifs of psycho-analytical criticism. In Freudian terms, the poet is looked upon as a day-dreamer, who publishes his phantasies and is, thus, strangely socially validated. These phantasies are supposed to be based on childhood experiences and complexes and can be symbolised also in dreams, in myths and fairy tales. Literature, thus, contains a rich storehouse of evidence for man's sub-conscious life. Freud derived the name of the Oedipus complex from a play by Sophocles—*Oedipus Rex* or *Oedipus the King* and interpreted *Hamlet* and *The Brothers Karmazov* as allegories of incestuous love and hatred. But Freud did not have a deep interest in literature and always recognized that psycho-analysis did not solve the question of art. His followers have, however, applied his methods systematically to an interpretation of literature. Psychology impinges on the province of the literary critic in the study of human experience and behaviour. As Herbert Read has suggested, in such a situation, the critic should retaliate and pick up from the science of psychology his brightest weapons.[15] Richards belongs to the school of psychological criticism like Herbert Read. Richards is fully justified in borrowing from the science of psychology his critical vocabulary and tools of analysis. Wimsatt and Brooks are fully justified in describing I.A. Richards as "the critic through whose mediation psychology was to make its greatest impact upon literary criticism."[16] In an interview, Richards described himself as "someone really saturated in psychology and neurology, making up a book about the literary approaches."[17] For him it was a bit of luck really, for two quite different concerns or studies were crossing at a crucial point to provide him with tools for an interdisciplinary work in *Principles of Literary Criticism.* As a critic, Richards is concerned with the analysis of the experiences stimulated by a work of art.

A third trend of twentieth century criticism could be called linguistic. It takes seriously the famous saying of Mallarmé that poetry is not written with ideas but with words. Poetry is a form of language. Richards may be assigned to this linguistic trend of criticism because of his profound interest in language—in the behaviour of words and semantics. He has developed views about the nature of poetic meaning or emotive language as contrasted with scientific meaning or intellectual language. His views have considerable influence on the whole modern critical movement. The Richardsian semantic analysis has had an important influence on several American critics who are usually called the New Critics. Notable critics in this mode are Cleanth Brooks, Robert Penn Warren, Allen Tate, John Crowe Ransom, William Empson, R.P. Blackmur and William K. Wimsatt. The New Critics concentrate exclusively on the language of poetry and account for its structure in terms of the layers of meaning the words are charged with. New Criticism is generally, taken to encompass the work of T.S. Eliot and I.A. Richards.

René Wellek called the fourth type of twentieth century criticism the new organistic and symbolist formalism. This organistic formalism has many antecedents. It started in the theories of German transcendalists late in the eighteenth century. The German metaphysical and transcendental ideas formulated by Kant, Fichte, Schelling and Schiller came to England with Coleridge. His *Biographia Literaria* has been described by Richards as "that lumber-room of neglected wisdom, which contains more hints towards a theory of poetry than all the rest ever written upon the subject."[18] Through devious channels many of its ideas entered the theories of French symbolism late in the nineteenth century and more directly. As René Wellek has noted, "from Hegel and De Sanctis his organistic formalism found an impressive formulation in the aesthetics of Benedotte Croce. Coleridge's, Croce's and Freud's symbolism are the immediate antecedents of modern English and American so-called New Criticism. This tradition of criticism is idealistic in its philosophical assumptions. But strangely and surprisingly this tradition combined here with the positive psychology and utilitarian semantics of I.A. Richards."[19]

If Freud stimulated the psychological school of criticism in his stress on psycho-analytic study of literature, Carl Jung, in contrast to Freud, with his psychiatric analysis, promoted the growth of Myth Criticism. It appeals to the results of cultural anthropology and the speculations of Carl Jung. Jung affirms that the unconscious mind is capable at times of assuming an intelligence and purposiveness which are superior to actual conscious insight.

According to Jung, "A great work of art is like a dream." He claimed a parallelism between poem and dream. "The poem presents an image in much the same way as nature allows a plant to grow, and we must draw our own conclusions."[20] Jung's concept of racial memory and the collective unconscious and his notion of "arche types"—images which derive their power from their long history in the collective unconscious, proved to be especially fruitful for literary criticism. Maud Bodkin's book *Archetypal Patterns of Poetry* (1934) investigated some of the ways in which these primodial images and situations recounted for the impact made by certain great works of literary art.

Richards's theory of poetry is to be studied in the context of the different schools of criticism mentioned earlier. The sixth major trend of modern criticism, indicated by René Wellek in his *Concepts of Criticism*, inspired by existentialism, does not have much relevance for an investigation into Richards's conception of poetry.

NOTES

1. Derek Hudson ed., *English Critical Essays*, Twentieth century, p. 34.
2. Johnson, Samuel, The Six Chief Lives from *Lives of the Poets*, (Macmillan, London, 1940), p. 171.
3. T.S. Eliot, *The Use of Poetry and the Use of Criticism*, p. 77.
4. Arthur Symons in introduction to *Biographia Literaria* (London, 1947), p. viii.
5. *Ibid.*, p. 151.
6. *Ibid.*, p. 150.
7. Derek Hudson, *op. cit.*, p. 35.
8. *Ibid.*
9. Matthew Arnold, *Essays in Criticism* (Second Series) (London, Macmillan, 1960), p. 1.
10. *Ibid.*
11. *Ibid.*, p. 2.
12. *Ibid.*
13. René Wellek, *Concepts of Criticism*, p. 346.
14. *Ibid.*, p. 348.
15. Herbert Read, *Collected Essays in Literary Criticism,* Faber and Faber, London, 1938, p.13.

16. Wimsatt and Brooks, *op.cit.*, p. 613.
17. Reuben Brower et al., ed. *I.A. Richards : Essays in His Honor*, OUP, New York, 1973, p. 28.
18. *Principles of Literary Criticism.*
19. René Wellek, *op. cit.*, p. 354.
20. Carl Jung, *Modern Man in Search of a Soul*, (tr. Dell and Beynes), New York, 1934, p. 198.

The Background of I.A. Richards's Literary Criticism

2

I.A. Richards's critical writings are rooted in the intellectual milieu in which he found himself in this age of science and technology. In the words of Denys Thompson, "The arts in the twenties seemed to attract but little of the available human talent; it was the science that engaged the attention of the able and established an arena within which important things happened."[1]

In an interview Richards told Brower that he first developed an interest in poetry when he was "laid up all my early teens with T.B." Richards says, "I had unlimited leisure. I read and read. Suddenly I got engulfed by Kipling".[2] The word "Dolores" used by Swinburne stirred up his imagination and led him to *The Battle Chorus from Frechthens*. Richards confesses, "I didn't know what was going to send me, after many days, to the Iliad. But the Frechthens stood by me. At fearsome moments it was a talisman to restore courage and it took me to Cambridge."[3]

As advised by C.K. Ogden (four years his senior), he "went into moral sciences" and then he tells us, "I got enthralled by G.E. Moore." Richards acknowledges that Moore was a "key-point" in the development of his critical ideas. He confesses, "I don't think I ever understood anything. But it was complete subjugation. I got really interested in language because I felt something must be done to stop the leakage of information that was going on there all the time. I know I didn't understand Moore or what he was at. I always thought if I went back to him for a whole course of lectures once again an inkling would come."[4]

The beginning of neo-realism is traced in the writings of George Edward Moore. He leads the revolt of British empiricism and common sense realism against German transcendentalism and absolutism. As a professor of Cambridge, he has influenced by his teachings and writings, the course of philosophical thinking in England in a unique way and brought into existence the realistic outlook of thought, sometimes called 'Cambridge Philosophy.' Richards was deeply stirred by G.E Moore's refutation of Idealism. He was particularly influenced by G.E. Moore's *Principia Ethica and Ethics*. In *Principles of Literary Criticism,* Richards led that attack upon Idealism, particularly the idealism of F.H. Bradley, which first won for Moore and Russell their reputation as philosophers. Richards, however, does not accept the point of view advocated by G.E. Moore in *Principia Ethica* and *Ethics* that an experience described as good is endowed with a certain ethical property or attitude not to be reduced to any psychological properties or attributes. It appears, on the whole, under the impact of G.E. Moore's refutation of Idealism, Richards was driven to revolt against Metaphysical and Idealistic Aesthetics of Immanuel Kant.

As already noted, Richards himself had studied not English literature but philosophy. He obtained a first class in the Moral Science Tripas in 1915 and returned to Cambridge as college lecturer in English and Moral Science at his own college, Magdalene, in 1921. In the second term of that year he gave a course of lectures on the novel. In the first and second terms of 1922, he gave courses on the theory of criticism and again in the first term of 1924. What we have been calling modern criticism began in 1924 with the publication of *Principles of Literary Criticism.* It proved to be a book of seminal importance. In the words of Joan Bennett, "It was valuable at that time to be presented with a basis for literary criticism, rational, man-centred, rooted in utilitarianism."[5] In *Principles of Literary Criticism*, Richards always raises the basic question: "How does poetry or imaginative literature in general contribute to the good of man?" Richards's own ideas about poetry had been nurtured by the study of moral philosophy from Plato and Aristotle to John Stuart Mill and G.E. Moore. With my limited understanding I am not competent to guess what each of these thinkers contributed towards Richards's own formulations of ideas. But it is clear that his thought was permeated by questions raised and answered in terms of ethical value. Richards's theory of value is based on his version of prudential and ethical codes. It bears a very close resemblance to utilitarianism of John Stuart Mill and Jeremy Bentham. According to the greatest happiness principle, advocated by Mill, "the ultimate end is an experience exempt as far as possible from pain, and as rich as possible in enjoyment both in point of quality and quantity."[6] Curiously enough, Mill's line of thinking is basically similar to that of Richards. The only difference that is to be noted is that in his psychological theory of values, Richards uses words like "satisfaction of impulses", "frustration of impulses" and "importance" in place of "enjoyment," "pain" and "quality."

In its stress on 'the good of man and/or utility to mankind,' Richards's theory of art and poetry is frankly utilitarian. His value-theory of the arts is based on a frank acceptance of utilitarian prudential ethics. His aesthetic thinking has a pragmatic bias. In his writings, Richards refers to Frege Charles Pierce, William James and John Dewey. William James claims that pragmatism is nothing new. The term 'Pragmatism' is derived from the same Greek word 'pragma' meaning action, from which the words 'practice' and 'practical' come. It was first introduced into philosophy by Charles Pierce in 1978. Pierce holds that our beliefs are really rules for our action. To develop the meaning of thought we need only determine what conduct it is fitted to produce. Pragmatism is as old as the surprising Greeks. While Socrates initiated it, Aristotle used it methodically. Richards is deeply influenced by the instrumentalism of John Dewey. Richards is stirred by Pierce's laboratory habit of mind and James's biological outlook and experimental method in philosophy. Under the impact of the philosophy of pragmatism, there was a gradual transformation of faith from the idealism of Plato to experimentalism.

Richards shows a vital interest in theories about the influence of language upon the way in which we think, and a concern with how much we fail in communicating verbally with one another and the reasons for this. These are the fundamental motives of Richards's writings. *The Meaning of Meaning* by Ogden and Richards deals with the influence of language upon the way in which we think. It appeared at a crucial stage in the development of modern logic. In the early twenties, there was a widespread concern with the influence of language upon philosophical theories. There was an attempt to create an ideal language with the aid of a reformulated logic. The new version had been proposed in 1918 by Bertrand Russell in his lectures on *The Philosophy of Logical Atewism* and in 1922 by Wiltgenstein's *Tractatus-Logico-Philosophicus*. The publication of Wiltgenstein's work in 1922 had initiated a movement which was making itself felt in the wider philosophical circles and generating new problems which had to be met. Ogden and Richards took the scientific study of language under the influence of logical positivism. They were inspired by Wiltgenstein's book. As Wiltgenstein himself tells us, the whole meaning of the Tractatus can be summed up as follows: "What can be said at all can be said clearly, and whereof one cannot speak thereof one must be silent."[7] Ogden and Richards propose an "analytical philosophy." They declare philosophy and aesthetics to be "the examination of the ways in which language is used." In many philosophies of language it is assumed, either explicitly or implicitly, that language has but two functions, namely the indicative and the evocative or emotive—any primary representative function, either intuitive or symbolic, being denied on the assumption of dual function of language. Thus, a critique of language is undertaken which involves vital issues for philosophy. "The entire philosophy of language of Ogden and Richards is based upon these premises and is also a cardinal assumption of the so-called Vienna School being explicitly asserted by Carnap."[8]

Ogden and Richards are primarily concerned with the psychology of language and its functions as a social and cultural phenomenon. Employing the empirical criteria of 'meaning' as formulated by logical positivism, Richards finds a meaning of distinguishing the meaningful from the unmeaning in language, apparent words from real words, pseudo-sentences from real sentences. It is in this context that Richards comes to describe poetry as "pseudo-statement" in *Science and Poetry*.

Before turning to literary criticism, Richards has actually done some fundamental thinking with ultimate things, thought and words, and the meaning of meaning. No doubt, it was at first his training in psychology which gave the new and exploratory flavour to all he said. In an interview, Richards describes himself as "some one really saturated in psychology and neurology making up a book about the literary approaches; for him, it was a bit of luck really, for two quite different concerns or studies were crossing at a crucial point to provide him with the tools for an interdisciplinary work."[9] Richard's interest in the nervous system derives from his interest in neurology. He is frankly wedded to the Behaviorist way of thinking. He is deeply influenced by the Behaviorism of Watson and Pavlov. Richards's psychology breaks away from the set of ideas, by which popular and academic psychology alike attempt to describe the mind. The mind is conceived, in terms of transcendental idealism, as a thing of a peculiar spiritual kind, fairly persistent, though valuable, endowed with attributes, three in number, its capacities for willing, knowing and feeling. These three functions of the mind are supposed to be performed unconsciously as well as consciously. Richards accepts the identification of the mind in Behaviorism with the nervous system. He alleges that the recognition of this fact has been delayed in an extraordinary fashion by the prevalence, among psychologists, of persons with philosophic antecedents. With every advance of neurology since the First World War, the evidence becomes more overwhelming. As a psychologist, Richards accepts the validity of the researches of Behaviorists and psycho-analysts, but urges that "the assumptions and results of both needing to be corrected however in ways which the recent experimental and theoretical investigations of the 'Gestalt' school are indicating."[10] Richards accepts the behaviorist view that we are our bodies, especially our nervous systems, more especially still the higher or more central co-ordinating parts of it. According to it, the mind is a system of impulses. Richards contends that this view should not be described as Materialism. "It might equally well be called Idealism".[11] In Richards's view, neither of the terms—Materialism or Idealism, in this connection, has any scientific or any strictly symbolic meaning or reference. Both are emotive terms used to incite or support certain emotional attitudes. They do not stand for any separable, observable group of things or character in things. Like a logical positivist, Richard argues that the attempt to say what things are, is futile because the question is non-sensical. For some people, terms like 'Idealism' and 'Materialism' are used as emotive agents round which attitudes, aspirations and values are rallied. From Richards's point of view, the Mind-Body problem is, strictly speaking, no problem. Richards claims that if the mind is identified with a part of the working of the nervous system and if mental events are recognized as identical with certain neural events, no disturbance of anyone's attitude to the world, his fellow-men or to himself is involved apart from certain drastic changes in theological considerations. The nervous system is the stimuli by which stimuli from the environment or from within the body result in appropriate behaviour.[12] Richards defines an impulse as "the process in the course of which a mental event may occur, a process apparently beginning in a stimulus and ending in an act."[13] As Richards perceives it, "the organism is a delicate registering instrument. One of its functions is that of perceiving or registering the environment. Single impulses never occur in actual experience. Even the simplest human impulses are very intricate bundles of mutually dependent impulses, and in any actual human behaviour the number of simultaneous and connected impulses occurring is beyond estimation."[14] Psychology is concerned with complex impulse. All our activities are intricate. Stimuli are only received if they serve some need of the organism. The influence of Behaviorism colours Richards's conception of poetry. Richards, in his analysis of the reading of a poem in chapter XVI of *Principles of Literary Criticism*, studies the details of the procedure in connection with the use of words. Here he stresses the general principle that "to know anything is to be influenced by it, directly when we sense it, indirectly when the effects of past conjunctions of impressions come into play."[15]

Richards notes that as the tendencies awakened by a situation are various and different there is scope for conflict, suppression and interplay, all contributing something to our experience. He regrets that this aspect of experience as filled with incipient promptings, lightly stimulated tendencies to acts of one kind or another, faint preliminary preparations for doing this or that, has been constantly overlooked in criticism. "Yet it is in terms of attitudes, the resolution, inter-animation and balancing of impulses that all the most valuable effects of poetry must be described."[16] We may cite Aristotle's definition of tragedy as an instance to corroborate Richards's view.

Thus, we note that as a background to the later critical sections in *Principles of Literary Criticism*, Richards includes as a preliminary what amounts to a concise treatise on psychology. In his theory of criticism, he raises all the topics of psychology from an angle which ordinary textbooks do not contemplate. He claims to present a fresh, heterodox view of the mind. Contrary to received opinion, he insists "upon an account of knowledge in terms merely of the causation of our thoughts, but the details of the analysis of poetic experience, the account of imagery, of emotion, of pleasure, of incipient action and so forth, although no similar analysis has before been explicitly set out, may be taken as comparatively orthodox."[17]

In the chapter entitled "Analysis of a Poem", Richards frames an outline or scheme of the mental events which make up the experience of looking at a picture or 'reading a poem' and he lays down three important qualifications of a good critic. First, a good critic must be an adept of experiencing, without eccentricities, the state of mind relevant to the work of art he is judging. Secondly, he must be able to distinguish experiences from one another as regards their less superficial features. Thirdly, he must be a sound judge of values. As psychology, even in its present conjectural state, has a direct bearing upon all these matters, the critic should have clear ideas of the general psychological form of the experiences with which he is concerned.

He should have clear ideas as to the elements present or as to their relative importance. He should have an understanding of the problem structures of these experiences. Naturally, Richards's logical positivist, Benthamite, Utilitarian, Behaviorist, neurological and Pragmatic bias colours his conception of poetry.

NOTES

1. Reuben Brower et al. ed. *I.A. Richards: Essays in His Honor*, OUP, New York, 1973, p. 296.
2. *Ibid.*, p. 17.
3. *Ibid.*, p. 18.
4. *Ibid.*, p. 20.
5. *Ibid.*, p. 48.
6. John Stuart Mill, *Utilitarianism*, p. 17.
7. John Passmore, *A Hundred Years of Philosophy* (Jerald Duckworth, London, 1957), p. 354.
8. W.M. Urban, *Language and Reality* (George Allen & Unwin, London, 1951), p. 69.
9. Reuben Brower *op. cit.*, p. 28.
10. I.A. Richards, *Principles of Literary Criticism*, p. 83.
11. *Ibid.*, p. 84.
12. *Ibid.*, p. 85.
13. *Ibid.*, p. 86.
14. *Ibid.*
15. *Ibid.*, p. 90.
16. *Ibid.*, p. 113.
17. *Ibid.*, p. 82.

Richards on the Two Uses of Language

3

Auden describes poetry as "memorable speech". Since poetry is a form of speech, a distinctive way of the employment of language, our discussion of Richards's theory of poetry should start with a discussion of the function of language. Such discussion has a tendency to have a philosophic temper. Richards pinpoints this problem in his *Practical Criticism*: "we are all in danger of becoming philosophers as soon as we attempt to explain our use of words or draw distinctions between our thoughts."[1] W.M. Urban has shrewdly noted, "Language is the last and deepest problem of the philosophic mind."[2] All life comes back to the question of our speech, the medium through which we communicate. Great writers like Henry James think so. Even a direct apprehension or intuition of life, the meaning of life, cannot be communicated except in language of some kind. Such transmission or communication is the part of the life-process itself. Hence, it is that as Urban states, "Philosophical enquiry into the origin and nature of language is as old as that into the essence and origin of being."[3] It is not a matter of surprise, therefore, that reflection on language is one of the oldest and most constant pre-occupations of the human mind. Turning to India, we note that the seers of the Upanishads exhort us to meditate on speech. Contemporary interest in problem of language has stimulated investigation by philosophers, psychologists and linguists into such question as the nature of communication and interpretation, the relation of logic to grammar, the part played by conventions in determining the boundaries of intelligible discourse, the number and kinds of distinct functions of language and the relation of all these questions both to each other and to some of the major problems of philosophy.

In *The Meaning of Meaning*, Richards and Ogden announce a new "Science of Symbolism" which provides a definite basis for scientific aesthetics. I venture to suggest that this line of thinking in *The Meaning of Meaning* leads to Richards's scientific conception of poetry. According to Ogden and Richards, all language is symbolic. Words mean nothing by themselves. It is only when a thinker makes use of them that they stand for anything, or, in one sense, have meaning. As instruments or symbols, they direct and organize, record and communicate. In stating what they direct and organize, record and communicate, we have to distinguish between Thoughts and Things.[4] As both the words "thing" and "object" have an unfair history, Ogden and Richards find it desirable to introduce a technical term to stand for whatever we may be thinking of or referring to. In the idiom of Ogden and Richards, the word 'referent' has been adopted to stand for the object of thought or the thing referred to in a particular discourse.

The lack of consideration of these elements in the language situation raises problems and difficulties which vanish when the whole transaction is considered in greater detail. Ogden and Richards introduce, at this state, in their system of thought, the distinction between the two uses of language. The belief that words stand for things or referents is at the core of the referential use of language and the referential use should be paramount for all reflective, intellectual use of language. "But", Ogden and Richards go on to indicate, "words have other functions which may be grouped together as emotive."[5] Ogden and Richards contend that the importance of the emotive aspect of language cannot be minimized. In fact, the study of such aspects has a paramount importance for those chiefly concerned with popular or primitive speech. The authors stress the magic of words in the context of the theories of the naturalistic origin of language. They point to "a certain bewitchery or fascination in words which makes them operate with a force beyond what can naturally give account of." In Anatole Francis' *Revolt of the Angels,* young Maurice's guardian angel exclaims: "And what is human language but the cry of the beasts of the forest or the mountains, complicated and corrupted by arrogant anthropoids."[6] From the naturalistic point of view, language consists of "the sounds of the forest and the mountain—a series of squeaks and grunts." Ogden and Richards have noted carefully that the primeval origin of language are reflected in its structure even in present times. "Tens of thousands of years have elapsed since we shed our tails, but we are still communicating with a medium developed to meet the needs of arboreal man."[7] This primitive linguistic outlook persists on the form of the attribution of magical powers to names and in the alluring tendency to hypostatization. The authors deplore the persistence of such verbal superstitions in the work of the profoundest thinkers. They allege that the philosophy of the nineteenth century was dominated by an idealist tradition in which the elaboration of master's symbolic machinery was substituted for direct research and occupied the centre of attention.[8] They find a serious defect in the Hegelian dialectic for its lack of a sound theory of language.

The earlier writers are full of the relics of primitive word-magic. For magic, the name of a thing or a group of things is its soul. The doctrine of the logos is variously conceived as the supreme reality, the divine soul substance. In the *Symposium* and the *Phaedo*, Plato has evolved a realm of pure ideality, also described as physis, in which these name-souls dwell, pure, divine, immortal, intelligible, uniform, indissoluble and unchangeable.[9] It was Heraclitus, the Greek philosopher, who first appealed to words as embodying the nature of things. His influence on Plato is manifest in the *Cratylus*. Ogden and Richards rightly deplore the neglect of this dialogue of Plato which contains his views on language. *Cratylus* has as its central theme the problem of the natural rightness of names which resolves itself into the fundamental problem of linguistic validity on the relation of language to reality. Richards commends Plato's scientific approach to the problem of names and their meaning in an age when comparative philology, grammar and psychology were all unknown. But Richards perceives Plato's failure to distinguish consistently between symbols and the thought symbolised.

The symbolic use of language naturally leads to the emotional aspects of the use of language. Turning to the more emotional aspects of modern thought, Ogden and Richards, in *The Meaning of Meaning,* find in it "a veritable orgy of verbo-mania." Even the sign of Divinity, as William James points out, has been slowly reduced to a "conglomeration of attributes, purely or almost purely verbal."[10] The verbal husk has a certain bombic capacity, an affective resonance which enables the manipulation of symbols such as the Absolute to assure himself that his labours are not altogether vain. "When language is once grown familiar," says Berkeley, "the hearing of the sounds or sights of the characters is often immediately attended with those passions which at first were wanted to be produced by the intervention of ideas that are now quite omitted." We thus pass to the emotive use of words from a consideration of its symbolic use. With regard to the words so used, as in poetry, Ribot has well remarked that they no longer act as signs but as sounds, they are musical notes at the service of an emotional psychology. "All sounds," says Yeats, "evoke indefinable and yet precise emotions." Byron in *The Childe Harold* hopes that "there may be words which are things." It is not surprising that a consideration of the ways in which language has been made to serve mankind in the past should lead to a special reaction and "a low elevation of language", as Urban puts it. Ogden and Richards, therefore, sound a note of warning that words may come between us and our objects in countless subtle ways if we do not realise the nature of their power. The best means of escape from scepticism or linguistic nihilism as well as from the hypnotic influences of word-magic lies in a clear realization of the way in which symbols come to exercise such power and of the various senses in which they are said to have meaning.[11] The authors recognize the significance of Cassiner's *Philosophy of Symbolic Forms* (1923) in the survey of man's progress towards verbal independence.

While presenting the theory of definition, Ogden and Richards draw our attention to two distinct uses or functions of language. In actual discussion, terms are used at least as much as for the sake of their sensory and emotive effects as for their strictly symbolic value. It is often imperative to decide whether a particular use of symbols is primarily symbolic or emotive. This is especially the case with certain kinds of metaphor. Ogden and Richards draw our attention to the cry of the psalmist; "They have sharpened their tongues like a serpent, adders' poison is under their lips." Richards finds it hard to determine whether an elusive similarity between the reptile and the persons described by the psalmist enables him figuratively to state something by them, or whether the sole function of the utterance is to express his emotion, i.e. to express his abhorrence of them and to promote rhetorically similar attitudes towards them in his hearers.

A consideration of the problem of Beauty is, perhaps, the best introduction to the question of the diverse functions of language. Even in the best critics, we find sentences which it is impossible to understand in the same way as we endeavour to understand those of physiologists. There is a common and important use of words which is different from the scientific or the strictly symbolic use. Richards introduces, in this context, the convenient division between the symbolic and the emotive use of words. Ogden and Richards proceed to comment thus on the two uses of language: "The symbolic use of words is statement; the recording, the support, the organization and the communication of references. The emotive use of words is a more simple matter, it is the use of words to express or excite feelings and attitudes. It is probably more primitive".[12] When, for instance, we say 'Hurrah' or 'Poetry is a spirit', or, 'Man is a worm', we are most probably using words merely to evoke certain attitudes.

As Ogden and Richards clearly indicate, each of these contrasted functions of language has two sides, that of the speaker and that of the listener. Under the symbolic function are included both the symbolization of reference and its communication to the listener, i.e. the causing in the reader of a similar reference. Under the emotive function are included both the expression of emotions, attitudes, moods, intentions, etc. in the speaker and their communication, i.e. their evocation in the listener. It is true that some element of reference probably enters for all civilized adults at least, into almost all use of words and it is always possible to impart a reference, if it be only a reference to things in general. The two functions of language distinguished in Richards's thought-system are subtly interwoven or intermingled in the usual course but, nevertheless they are in principle distinct. Richards, along with Ogden, pleads for a constant and conscious understanding of the duality of the symbolic and emotive functions of language. "The best test of whether our use of words is essentially symbolic or emotive is the question: Is this true or false in the ordinary strict scientific sense? If this question is relevant then the use is symbolic, if it is clearly irrelevant then we have an emotive utterance."[13] This brings Richards to the question of the distinctive use of language in poetry. "Very much poetry consists of statements, symbolic arrangements capable of truth or falsity, which are used not for the sake of the attitudes which their acceptance will evoke, the most important function of emotive language is fulfilled, and any symbolic function that the words may have is instrumental only and subsidiary to the evocative function."[14] This involves two distinct levels of truth. From this point of view, what is true for symbolic or referential purposes is different from what is true for emotive purposes. $\text{Tr}\overset{S}{\text{u}}\text{e}$ and $\text{Tr}\overset{E}{\text{u}}\text{e}$ are different symbols.

Ogden and Richards plead for a general consciousness of the nature of the two functions of language if they are to be kept from interfering with each other. In particular, all the verbal disguises, by which each at times endeavours to pass itself off as the other, need to be expressed. Any scientific statement can at best be more general or more useful than another but it cannot pretend to give a more inspiring or more profound vision of reality than another. From this point of view, it ought to be impossible to talk about poetry or religion as though they were capable of giving 'knowledge,' especially since 'knowledge' as a term has been so overworked from both sides that it is no longer of much service.[15]

The perception of the dual function of language provides the key to Richards's aesthetic thinking in *The Meaning of Meaning* which provides a precise and succinct summary of Richards' achievement in the field of aesthetics. In this book, Richards, like Matthew Arnold before him, brackets poetry with religion as a subject in which the evocation of feelings, emotions and attitudes, has the primary significance. We may cite, in this context, Arnold's view stated in *The Study of Poetry* that in the age of the advancement of scientific knowledge, religion is losing its power and that poetry will become a substitute for religion. As Richards perceives the situation, religions have so persistently and so definitely exploited the confusion of the dual function of language and are so dependent upon this muddle that they are to be conceived unmistakably as pathological growths. Richards indicates sharply that a poem or a religion has no concern with limited and directed reference. From Richards's point of view, a poem "tells us or should tell us, nothing. It has a different, though an equally important and a far more vital function— to use an evocative term in connection with an evocative matter. What it does or should do, is to induce a fitting attitude to experience".[16] The term 'fitting' is preferred to the term 'valuable' as being more precise. This is not to imply any narrow code of the proper attitudes to be adopted upon all occasions. Richards clarifies that the term 'attitude' should throughout this discourse be understood in a wider sense as covering all the ways in which impulses may be set ready for action, including these peculiar settings, from which no overt action results, often spoken of as the aesthetic moods or the aesthetic emotions. "But such words as 'fitting,' 'suitable,' 'appropriate,' are chilly, having little or no evocative power. Therefore, those who care most for poetry and who understand its central and crucial value tend to resent such language as unworthy of its subject."[17] Ogden and Richards, in *The Meaning of Meaning*, have used such terms with chilly associations to give a strictly symbolic or scientific description of the function of poetry. But once a general consciousness of the nature of the two functions of language is developed, it will be plain that the description of poetry, which is for many reasons the supreme form of the emotive use of language, in the light of recent developments a scientific knowledge, "cannot conflict with the poetic or evocative appraisal of poetry, with which poets as poets are concerned."[18] Richards, in this way, apologises for, or justifies his attempt to provide a strictly symbolic or scientific description of the function of poetry. Richards's sermon is that the legitimate functions of language should not be confused. The exercise of one function need not in any way interfere with the exercise of the other. One need not be irritated with the pretensions of scientific knowledge because one cares for poetry. D.H. Lawrence's passionate cry: "Whatever the sun may be, it is certainly not a ball of flaming gas," is an outburst against the cold philosophy of science. Scientists need not be totally immune from the influence of civilization by developing a resistance to literary values. Richards proposes a bifurcation of the functions of language. "As science frees itself from the emotional outlook, and modern physics is becoming something in connection with which attitudes seem rather detrop, so poetry seems to return to its conditions of its greatness by abounding the obsession of knowledge and symbolic truth."[19] This is the hope for poetry that Richards cherishes in *Science and Poetry* (later re-issued as *Poetries and Sciences*) and his later writings. Richards reminds us that it is not necessary to know what things are, in order to take up fitting attitudes towards them and the peculiarity of the greatest attitudes which art can evoke in their extraordinary width. Richards and Ogden regard the description and ordering of such attitudes as "the business of aesthetics." "The evaluation of such attitudes must rest ultimately upon the opinions of those best qualified to be judged by the range and delicacy of their experience and their freedom from irrelevant pre-occupations."[20] Those who regard interpretation as a purely casual process consider that when the meaning of anything is interpreted, it is but explained in casual terms. At the same time, they should organize a totally distinct sense of meaning in which the 'meaning' of a poem or religion would be the emotion or attitude evoked through it.[21] Thus, in terms of his own symbolic logic, Richards could very well anticipate the objection to his own aesthetic theories from those who passionately care for poetry and the arts.

That language has multiple functions has to be recognized. However, it has two principal uses—the symbolic and the evocative. Most writing or speech is governed by a compromise between the two principal functions of language. The mixed or rhetorical kind of writing or speech is opposed to the pure or scientific, or strictly symbolic use of words. Instances of the dropping of one or more of the language functions lead naturally to the most remarkable and most discussed case of such variation, the distinction, namely, between the prose and the poetic uses of language. Richards points out that the distinction is not happily symbolised in these terms, since poetry is best defined for the most general and most important purposes by relation to the state or states of mind produced in the 'poem' in suitable readings and without any relation to the precise verbal means. To Richards, the antithesis of symbolic and emotive uses of language is preferable to an antithesis of prose and poetry. In strictly symbolic language the emotional effects of the words, whether direct or indirect, are irrelevant to their employment. In evocative language, on the other hand, all the means by which the attitudes, moods, desires, feelings and emotions, can be verbally incited in an audience, are concerned. The matter is thus succinctly summed up: "In symbolic speech the essential considerations are the correctness of symbolization and the truth of the reference. In evocative speech the essential consideration is the character of the attitude aroused. Symbolic statement may indeed be used as a means of evoking attitudes but when this use is occurring, it will be noticed that the truth or falsity of the statements is of no consequence, provided that they are accepted by the hearer."[22] The appeal of poetry is mainly sensory in character. Milton had insisted that poetry should be sensuous. As Richards and Ogden endeavour to present a sort of scientific description of the indirect means of arousal which are possible through words used in poetry, they find it very necessary to insist upon the importance of the distinction between the scientific and emotive functions of language, in view of the prevailing misconceptions about the functions and uses of speech. Confusion between them, the authors warn us, leads to wrangles in which Intellect and Emotion, Reason and Feeling, Logic and Intuition, are set in artificial opposition to one another. The analysis of meaning in primitive language, conducted by Dr. M. Alinouster, confirms and re-enforces the confusion of Ogden and Richards that no theory of meaning can be given without the study of the mechanism of reference. In its primitive uses, language functions as a mode of action and as a piece of human behaviour and not as an instrument of reflection. It is only in the certain very special uses that language is employed to frame and express thoughts. In poetic and literary productions, language is made to embody human feelings and passions, to render in a subtle and convincing manner, states and processes of mind. In the critical writings of Richards, the study of the evocative aspects of language leads naturally to an account of the resources of poetical language and of the means by which it may be distinguished from symbolic or scientific statement. Thus, the technique of symbolism, as formulated by Ogden and Richards, is one of the essential instruments of the aesthetics of literature.[23] Bertrand Russell in his review of *The Meaning of Meaning* commends it because its methods and theories are scientific, not mythical.[24] The philosophy of language formulated in *The Meaning of Meaning* has a scientific orientation. John Crowe Ransom has noted significantly in *The New Criticism* that in this book Richards's philosophy of language was wide and not primarily aesthetic. *The Meaning of Meaning* is not primarily a book on aesthetic theory. As Ransom shrewdly remarks, "it rather incidentally legislates a status for poetry. Its bias is deeply nominalist and it is very alert to the possibility that a word which seems to refer to the objective world, or to have an objective referent, really refers to a psychological context and has no objective referent. This bias has governed Richards's conception of poetry, for one thing, almost from that day to this."[25] To quote Ransom once again, "*The Meaning of Meaning* is in terms of the new philosophy of language, the authors refer to the latter as symbolism, but since their book the name of it appears to have become standardized as semantics."[26] In fact, this scholarly work is based on a thorough survey of the history of semantic philosophy and on a critical examination of the requirements of effective symbolic communication. As we have seen, in *The Meaning of Meaning*, Richards makes a crucial commitment to a theory or philosophy of language which has a significant bearing on his conception of poetry. His interest in *The Meaning of Meaning*, in semantics, has proved his most fruitful contribution to criticism proper.

In *The Meaning of Meaning*, Richards, in collaboration with Ogden, announced a manifesto which launched a programme. In *The Principles of Literary Criticism* (1924), he applies to artistic theory the same treatment as *The Meaning of Meaning* had applied to the question of meaning. In *The Principles of Literary Criticism*, Richards endeavours to provide for the emotive foundation of language the same critical foundation as *The Meaning of Meaning* had attempted for the symbolic. In *The Principles of Literary Criticism* and his later writings, Richards develops and elaborates his observations on the two uses or distinct functions of language. When Richards wrote *The Principles of Literary Criticism*, the theory of language was one of the most neglected of all studies. According to Richards, a clear comprehension of the differences between the two totally distinct uses of language is indispensable for the theory of poetry and for the narrower aim of understanding much that is said about poetry. Richards proceeds to examine the mental processes which accompany these uses of language. Unfortunately, most of the psychological terms which we naturally employ, 'knowledge', 'belief', 'assertion', 'thought' and 'understanding', tend to blur the distinction, as the ambiguous use of these terms is not taken into consideration.

In his accounts of the mind, Richards substitutes the causes, the characters and the consequences of a mental event for its aspects as thought, feeling and will. Richards distinguishes between the two sets of causes of mental events. He first refers to the present stimuli reaching the mind through the sensory nerves in association with the effects of past stimuli and secondly to the state of the organism, its needs, its readiness to respond to some sort of stimulus. The impulses which arise are determined by the interaction of these two sets of causes.

In Richardsian terms, the impulse owing its character to its stimulus is described as reference. This stands for the property of mental events which we substitute for thought or cognition. But reference is distorted in some degree by the independent internal conditions of the organism. To a great extent, reference is interfered with by the needs and desires of the organism. We should be able to demarcate the fields where impulses should be, as completely as possible, dependent upon, and correspondent with external situation from those in which reference is subordinated to appetencies. In certain cases, reference should take prior place; in others, it is subordinated to appetencies. Reference is often subordinate to emotional satisfaction. Even the most ordinary and familiar objects are perceived as it pleases us to perceive.

In the present context of the phenomenal advancement of scientific knowledge, there has been an immense extension of our powers of referring. Science is autonomous. "So far as any body of reference is undistorted, it belongs to science."[27] Richards contends that sometimes advantage is gained from distortion of references. As Richards point out, "just as there are innumerable human activities which require undistorted references if they are to be satisfied, so there are innumerable other activities not less important which equally require distorted references or, more plainly, fictions."[28] Richards defends the imaginative use of fictions as being perfectly compatible with the fullest and grimmest recognition of the exact state of affairs on all occasions. It is no make-believe, the imaginative use of fictions is not a way of hoodwinking ourselves.

Richards affirms that "to be forced by desire into any unwarrantable belief is a calamity."[29] He is critical of the common misuse of fictions, for the state which ensues is often extraordinarily damaging to the mind. But these beliefs are capable of rendering us immense services, "provided we do not take them for what they are not, degrading the chief means by which our attitudes to actual life may be adjusted into the materials of a long-drawn delirium."[30] If we know enough, we could obtain all necessary attitudes through scientific references alone. In view of the inadequacy of the present state of our knowledge, this very remote possibility is best left alone.

Fictions may be aroused by statements or by analogous things in other arts. While fictions may be used in general to deceive, this is not a characteristic use of fictions in poetry. The use of language does not set up fictions in opposition to verifiable truths in the scientific sense. The scientific use of language consists in the use of a statement for the sake of the reference, true or false, which it causes. But it may also be used for the sake of the effects in emotion and attitude produced by the reference it occasions. This is the emotive use of language.[31] Richards makes a fervent plea for a clear grasp of this simple distinction between the two uses of language, "we may either use words for the sake of references they promote, or we may use them for the sake of the attitudes and emotions which ensue."[32] There are several arrangements of words which operate like musical phrases and evoke attitudes without any reference being required en-route. But usually references are involved as conditions for, or stages in, the ensuing development of attitudes, yet it is still the attitudes, not the references which are important. In such cases it does not matter whether the references are true or false. Their sole function is to bring about and support the attitudes which constitute the further response. To Richards, "the questioning, verificactory way of handling them is irrelevant, and in a competent reader it is not allowed to interfere."[33] Richards goes on to indicate that for scientific language a difference in the reference is itself failure, but for emotive language the widest differences in reference are of no importance if the further effects in attitude are of the required kind.

The two uses of language pre-suppose fundamental differences between the mental processes involved. There is a great difference in the notion of failure in each case. While for scientific language a difference in the reference is itself failure, as the end has not been attained; for emotive language even the widest differences in reference are irrelevant, unless the appropriate attitude and emotion are evoked. In the scientific use of language not only must the references be correct for success, but there must be logical connections and relations of references. But for emotive purposes logical arrangement is not necessary. In fact, it may be a source of obstacle. "For what matters," avers Richards, "is that the series of attitudes due to the references should have their own proper organization, their own emotional interconnection, and this often has no dependence upon the logical relations of such references as may be concerned in bringing the attitudes into being."[34]

Richards proceeds, in this context, to distinguish between the different meanings of the word 'truth' in criticism. In the scientific sense, a reference is true when things to which it refers are actually together in the way in which it refers to them, otherwise it is false. This sense of truth is very little in use in any of the arts. Though people continue to use the word 'Truth' with the same promiscuity as ever, the emotive power which attaches to the word is so great that it cannot be abandoned in general discussion. The second sense in which 'Truth' is most usually used is that of acceptability or internal necessity or rightness. Richards says, "That is 'true' or 'internally necessary' "which completes or accords with the rest of the experience, which co-operates to arouse our ordered response, whether the response of Beauty or another." The 'truth' of Daniel Defoe's "Robinsoe" is the acceptability of the things we are told, their acceptability is the interests of the effects of the narrative, not their correspondence with actual facts involving Alexander Selkerk or another."[35] When Keats exclaimed in "Ode on a Grecian Urn" that "Beauty is Truth, Truth Beauty", as an apprehension of the artistic beauty of the figures inscribed on the Grecian Urn, he was using the word "Truth" in the emotive sense to arouse feelings and attitudes. Again, when in his letters Keats affirmed, "what the imagination seizes as Beauty must be Truth", he was making an emotive or a poetic use of language.

According to Richards, "Poetry affords the clearest examples of the subordination of reference to attitude. It is the supreme form of emotive language."[36] It cannot be doubted that originally all language was emotive. Richards describes its scientific use as "a later development".[37] Though most language is still emotive, "yet the later development has come to seem the natural and the normal use, largely because the only people who have reflected upon the language were at the moment of reflection using it scientifically".[38]

NOTES

1. I.A. Richards, *Practical Criticism*, p. 327.
2. W.M. Urban, *Language and Reality*, London, 1951, p. 22.
3. *Ibid.*, p. 117.
4. Ogden and Richards, *The Meaning of Meaning*, p. 9.
5. *Ibid.*, p. 10.
6. Composed by W.M. Urban; *Language and Reality*, p. 57.

7. Ogden and Richards, *op. cit.*, p. 26.
8. *Ibid.*, p. 29.
9. *Ibid.*, p. 32.
10. *Ibid.*, p. 41.
11. *Ibid.*, p. 47.
12. *Ibid.*, p. 149.
13. *Ibid.*, p. 150.
14. *Ibid.*
15. *Ibid.*, p. 158.
16. *Ibid.*, pp. 158-59.
17. *Ibid.*, p. 159.
18. *Ibid.*
19. *Ibid.*
20. *Ibid.*
21. *Ibid.*, pp. 176-77.
22. *Ibid.*, p. 239.
23. *Ibid.*, p. 250.
24. William Wasserstem, ed., *A Dial Miscellany*, Syracuse University Press, 1963, p. 277.
25. John Crowe Ransom, *The New Criticism*, Norfolk, 1942, p. 5.
26. *Ibid.*
27. *Principles of Literary Criticism*, p. 266.
28. *Ibid.*
29. *Ibid.*
30. *Ibid.*, p. 267.
31. *Ibid.*
32. *Ibid.*
33. *Ibid.*, p. 268.
34. *Ibid.*
35. *Ibid.*, p. 269.
36. *Ibid.*, p. 273.
37. *Ibid.*
38. *Ibid.*

Richards's Definition of a Poem

4

As a background to the later critical sections in *The Principles of Literary Criticism*, Richards includes as a preliminary what amounts to a concise treatise of psychology. In his view of criticism, he discusses all the topics of psychology from an angle which ordinary textbooks do not contemplate. He claims to present a fresh, heterodox view of the mind. Accepting the behaviourist view, Richards contends that the mind is a system of impulses. Richards says, "the nervous system is the stimuli by which stimuli from the environment or from within the body result in appropriate behaviour."[1]

In terms of Richards's reconstruction of psychology, "the threefold division between the causes, character and consequences of a mental event, conscious or unconscious, corresponds, with certain qualifications, to the usual division in traditional psychology of thought (or cognition) feeling, and will (or cognition)."[2] Richards points out that the advantage of substituting the causation, the character and the consequences of a mental event as its fundamental aspects in place of its knowing, feeling and willing aspects is that instead of a trio of incomprehensible ultimates we have a set of aspects which not only mental events but all events share.[3] The nervous system is specialized to receive impressions through the organs of sense, but its state at any moment is also determined by a host of other factors such as the condition of blood and the position of the head. But, Richards admits, in the present state of the development of physiology and psychology "the relation between an awareness and what it is aware of, is a mystery."[4] Richards contends that "impressions are commonly signs, have effects which depend not on themselves alone but upon the other impressions which have co-operated with them in the past."[5] Following the relevant description in *The Meaning of Meaning*, he defines a sign as "something which has once been a member of a context or configuration that worked in the mind as a whole." Richards, in his analysis of the reading of a poem, in chapter XVI of *The Principles*, studies the details of the procedure in connection with the use of words. He lays down the general principle that to know anything is to be influenced by it, directly when we see it, indirectly when the effects of past conjunctions of impressions come into play.[6]

Wordsworth describes poetry "as the first and last of all knowledge."[7] Richards seeks to discover the type of knowledge that the reading of poetry can give. A theory of knowledge, from the Richardsian point of view, is indeed at the point, at which we wish to decide, whether a poem is true, or reveals reality, and if so, in what sense. This is admittedly a very important question. But a theory of feelings, of emotions, of attitudes and desires, of the affective-volitional aspect of human activity, is required at all stages of Richards's analysis.

"Poetry," says Dr. Johnson, "is the art of uniting pleasure with truth."[8] Richards has analyzed the different senses of "truth" in his study of "The Two Uses of Language." Now, what about "pleasure?" Richards objects to the loose use of the term "pleasure." He describes 'pleasure' in psychological terms as "successful activity of some kind not necessarily of a biologically useful kind." He describes unpleasure as "frustrated, chaotic mal-successful activity."[9] The quest for pleasure becomes an obsession with many individuals. From Richards's point of view, all those doctrines, very common in critical literature, are mistaken. Pleasure need not be looked upon as the ultimate goal of activity. Every activity has its own specific goal, pleasure is just a by-product. "To read a poem for the sake of true pleasure, which will ensue, if it is successfully read, is to approach it in an inadequate attitude."[10] We should be interested in the poem rather than in the by-product of having managed successfully to read it. Tragedy is often misapproached, for we think that a competent reader sits down to read it for the sake of pleasure. We have a poor psychological vocabulary. "Pleasure and unpleasure are our most delicate signs of how our activities are thriving."[11] Richards notes that "Wordsworth probably and Coleridge certainly, if they were to write today, would use quite other terms in place of pleasure for describing poetic values."[12]

Richards gives a scientific account of emotion as an ingredient of consciousness. Stimulating situations give rise to widespread ordered repercussions throughout the body, felt as clearly marked colourings of consciousness. These patterns in organic response are fear, grief, joy, anger and the other emotional states. These emotional states, with pleasure and unpleasure, are customarily distinguished under the head of feeling from sensations, which are very closely dependent for their character upon their stimulus. These sensations are ranked together as cognitive elements concerned, i.e. with our knowledge of things rather than with an attitude or behaviour towards them, or our emotion about them. From the Richardsian point of view, pleasure and emotion have also a cognitive aspect. According to Richards, "they give us knowledge; in the case of pleasure, of how our activities are going on, successfully or otherwise; in the case of emotion, knowledge primarily of our attitudes. But emotion may give us further knowledge."[13] There is no kind of mental activity in which memory does not intervene. The richness and complexity of experience is due to the apparent revival of past experience. "The interventions of memory are not confined to sensation and emotion. They are of equal importance in our active behaviour."[14]

According to Richards, "most behaviour is a reconconciliation between the various acts which would satisfy the different impulses which combine to produce it; and the richness and interest of the feel of it in consciousness depends upon the variety of the impulses engaged. Any familiar activity, when set in different conditions so that the impulses which make it up have to adjust themselves to fresh streams of impulses due to the new conditions, is likely to take an increased richness and fullness in consciousness."[15]

As Richards points out, "this general fact is of great importance for the arts, particularly for poetry, painting and sculpture, the representative or mimetic arts". The coordination of a great number of impulses of different kinds does not very often result in overt action. "There is a danger here of supposing that no action whatever results or that there is something incomplete or imperfect about such a state of affairs." Richards notes that the response required in many cases by works of art is of a kind which can only be obtained in an incipient or imaginal stage. Practical considerations often prevent their being worked out in overt form and Richards does not find the least reason to regret this, for these responses are commonly of the nature of solutions to problems, not of intellectual research, but of emotional accommodation and adjustment. Richards describes these imaginal and incipient activities or tendencies to action as attitudes. He notes that as the tendencies awakened by a situation are various and different, there is scope for conflict, suppression and interplay, all contributing something to our experience. He regrets that this aspect of experience, as filled with incipient promptings, lightly stimulated tendencies to acts of one kind or other, faint preliminary preparations for doing this or that, has been constantly overlooked in criticism. And yet, as Richards puts it, "it is in terms of attitudes, the resolution, inter-animation and balancing of impulses that all the most valuable effects of poetry must be described."[16] Aristotle's definition of tragedy, along with his theory of catharsis, is cited as an instance to corroborate Richards's view.

In the chapter entitled "The Analysis of a Poem," Richards frames an outline or scheme of mental events which make up the experience of looking at a picture or reading a poem. As Richards himself points out, much in his account of "The Poetic Experience" in *Poetries and Sciences* is a simplification of doctrines more elaborately expounded in *Principles of Literary Criticism.*[17] Richards begins by asking what kind of a thing in the widest sense, is poetry? In the light of the recent developments in psychology, it is at least possible to understand in general how the mind works in an experience and what sort of stream of events, the experience is. In "The Analysis of a Poem," Richards makes a diagrammatic representation of the events which take place when we read a poem. As the eye reads a succession of printed words, there follows a stream of reaction in which six distinct kinds of events may be distinguished—(1) the visual sensations of the printed words, (2) images very closely related with these sensations, (3) images relatively free, (4) reference to, or thinking of, various things, (5) emotions and (6) affective volitional attitudes. The impression of the printed words on the retina sets up an agitation which goes deeper and deeper. The sound of the words in the mind's ear and the feel of the words imaginatively spoken together give the full body, as it were, to the words. Next, various pictures arise "in the mind's eye," not of words but of things for which the words stand. These are described by Richards in *The Principles* as "tied images." Unlike the image bodies of the words themselves, those other images of things are not vitally important. For some, these tied images may be necessary, but other people may not require them at all. In their whole reaction to a poem or to a single line of it, their free images are the point at which the readings are most likely to differ. The stimulations from the reading of the poem find an immense hierarchy of systems of tendencies poised in the most delicate stability. The effect of grasping the literal sense of a word is immensely increased and widened when it is reinforced by fresh stimulation from tied images and it is through them that most of the emotional effects are produced.

The agitation caused by the experience of reading the poem divide into a major and minor branch. What Richards calls "the intellectual stream" is made up of thoughts, which are not static little entities that bob up into unconsciousness and down out of it, but fluent happenings, events which refer or point to the things the thoughts are of. But our thoughts which point to things are the servants of our interests. What Richards calls "The emotional stream" is made up of our interests. For those who do not genuinely love poetry, this intellectual stream of thoughts is what matters. But for passionate and genuine lovers of poetry, the active branch is what really matters; for from it the whole agitation comes. "Every Experience," in Richards's words, "is essentially some interest or group of interests swinging back to rest."[18] To indicate what an interest is, Richards pictures the mind as "a system of very delicate poised balances, a system which so long as we are in health is constantly growing."[19] The incredibly complex nature of the mind is imagined by Richards as an arrangement of several "magnetic needles, large and small, swung so that they influence one another, some able only to swing horizontally, others vertically, others hung freely."[20] The needles, from Richards's point of view, represent the nature of our multi-directional interests. Every new situation we have to face disturbs the balance among the needles to some extent, so that the whole assemblage of needles have to busily readjust themselves. The wagglings, which ensue as the system rearranges itself are our responses, the impulses through which we seek to meet the end. As Richards perceives it, the printed poem has to appeal to this incredibly complex assemblage of interests. It evokes an emotional response leading to the development of attitudes. Traditional Psychology stresses man's intellectual capacities but, in terms of Richards's view of psychology, intellect is an adjunct to the interests, a means by which they adjust themselves more successfully. Though intellect is what is distinctive in man, Richards asserts that "man is not primarily an intelligence, he is a system of interests. Intelligence helps man but does not run him."[21] As the mind is identified with the nervous system in Richards's behaviourist psychology, it is not to be treated as a directing intelligence but a system of multitudinous response. If the mind is the nervous system, Richards argues that as soon as we understand everything about the nervous system, we shall have an exact criterion for the evaluation of poetic experiences, for we shall be able to say what poetry agrees best with the nervous system and owes it good. Richards's immense faith in the future of neurology makes him adopt such a view of poetry. If the mind is pictured as an arrangement of magnetic needles interlinked and influencing one another, Richards points out that it is the function of poetry to bring such order among the needles that they cease from waggling and are at rest. To produce this harmonious, though fleeting, states of mind is the essential function of poetry. Any poetry can start them waggling, but only the best poetry can stop them from waggling.

In reading poetry, it is essential to give words their full imagined sound and body. Even before the words have been intellectually understood, the movement and sound of the words is playing deeply and intimately upon the interests. Though it has yet to be successfully investigated how this happens, no sensitive reader of poetry doubts it. A good deal of poetry and even some great poetry exists in which the sense of the words can be almost entirely missed or neglected without loss. But the relative importance of grasping the sense of words may vary. In nearly all poetry, the sound and feel of the words and the senses in which the words are later more explicitly taken, are subtly influenced by this fact. Richards points to the ambiguity of most words as regards their plain sense, especially in poetry. In the use of words most poetry is the reverse of science.

In his appraisal of poetry, Richards is primarily concerned with its meaning, "What is a meaning? What is it we are making out? are the master-keys to all the locked chambers and corridors of the theory of poetry open to us....."[22] Richards discovers several kinds of meaning in the study of literature or any other mode of communication. He observes in *Practical Criticism* "whether we are creative as in speech or writing, or passive, as readers or listeners, the Total Meaning we are engaged with is, almost always, a blend, a combination of several contributory meanings of different types. Language—and pre-eminently language, as it is used in poetry—has not one but several tasks to perform simultaneously."[23]

Richards proceeds upon a set of postulates. It is plain to him that most human utterances, and nearly all articulate speech can be profitably regarded from four points of view. He divides the meaning of a poem or any verbal expression into four aspects, (i) sense, or the logical content, the prose argument, which might be subject to fairly accurate paraphrase in prose; (ii) the feeling (about any or all of these within the poem) or the value contributed by the poet to the "state of affairs" set forth in the argument; (iii) tone, the attitude of the poet towards the reader, hostile, ingratiating, indifferent or the tone in which the reader is invited to respond, and (iv) intention (sum-total of the poet's guidance within the poem) or the aims the writer is trying to achieve.

Thus, as Richards explains, almost any utterance can be looked at from four points of view, revealing four kinds of meaning, though one or two may pre-dominate. As Denys Thompson has rightly noted, "these definitions are useful as eye-folds."[24] Even animals are capable of three kinds of meaning. Thus, a dog inside a gate may bark at a passer-by, and express feeling in the form of anger. The tone of the dog is contemptness of the passer-by, and the intention of the dog is to cause fear. As an example of the simplest human utterance, expletives usually have no sense, they express feeling and the tone varies with the audience, if any, and the intention is to relieve feeling, arouse sympathy with the speaker, and so on. It is true that the four kinds of meaning are not always easily separable, nor should every passage be approached with the idea of finding them, but they are indispensable terms for explaining with precision one's view on what has been read or heard.[25] Jereme P. Schiller has rightly observed that "sense," "feeling" and "tone" are nothing more than new names for the "strictly symbolic use," "the expression of attitude towards the things referred to" and "expression of attitude towards the audience" of *The Meaning of Meaning*. The "expression of intention" of that work, however, is broadened in *Practical Criticism* to include unconscious as well as conscious aims or effects.[26]

Meaning depends upon the manner, the tone of voice, the cadence and the rhythm of words and an accuracy is lent to poetical descriptions which is lacking in prose descriptions. Language, logically and scientifically used, cannot describe a landscape or a face.[27] In poetic use, a word, phrase or sentence may carry an indefinite number of possible sense. A prose-poet, like Ruskin or De Quincey, makes the reader pick out the precise particular senses required for a particular occasion.

Over-insistence on the thought in separation from the rest leads to a misunderstanding and under-estimation of poetry. "It is never what a poem says that matter but what it is. The poet is not writing as a scientist."[28] Words used in poetry are intended to communicate to a suitable reader "a similar play of interests putting him for the while into a similar situation and leading to the same response."[29] Speaking of the communicative value of poetry, Richards notes that "the words recording the poetic experience seem to become the cause of a similar experience in the mind of a suitable reader."[30]

II. THE DEFINITION OF POEM

In the chapter entitled "The Definition of a Poem," Richards touches once again upon the problem of the nature of the poetic experience. In defining a poem, he argues, we are misled by the superstition that there is something actual, the poem, which all readers have access to and upon which they pass judgment. But what does this poem stand for? Richards cautions us that most critical discussion is primarily emotive, with no precise formulations. While talking about a poem we may be talking about the artist's experience, such of it as is relevant, or about the experiences of a qualified reader who made no mistakes about an idea and perfect reader's possible experience, or about an actual experience. Most usually we mean by the poem the artist's experience or our own actual experience of the poem. We forget what communication is. In *The Meaning of Meaning*, Ogdèn and Richards have described "a communication or language transaction as a use of symbols in such a way that acts of reference occur in the hearer which are similar in all relevant respects to those which are symbolized by them in the speaker."[31] We may accept this definition of communication as a starting point. As all meaning involves reference, so all communication of meaning involves a similarity of reference in speaker and hearer.

There are, generally speaking, only two possible answers to the problem of intelligible communication. The first is the naturalistic or behaviouristic theory, and the second is the idealistic or the transcendental theory. The first, the naturalistic theory of communication is, to Richards, the simpler and on the face of it, the more plausible account of communication. This naturalistic theory is explicitly stated by Richards in chapter XXI of his *Principles of Literary Criticism*. It has a very definite bearing on Richards's introspection of the nature of poetry. According to Richards, the ideal or transcendental theory of communication is based on the definition of communication as the actual transference of experiences in the strictest possible sense of transference. Those who reject the naturalistic theory do not because of some mystical poetical conception of intermingling, or interpretation of minds or the belief that even "particular minds are merely an illusory experience of the underlying reality of one mind whose facets or aspects are many."[32] The transcendalists reject the simpler theory and accept the more involved, not on grounds of evidence but on grounds of desire, due to the influence of the contrary opinion or attitudes towards their fellows. It is admitted by Richards that if there were direct contact of mind with mind, if actual transference and participation did occur, we should, of course, be compelled to adopt the transcendental theory. "It does not occur," asserts Richards, "and no arguments which assure it have the least weight."[33] "On any identity on 'participation' theory, communication becomes an ineffable and incurable irreversible mystery."[34] "All that occurs," Richards goes on to assert, "is that, under certain condition, separate minds have closely similar experiences."[35] From Richards's point of view, belief in the actual contact between minds or in the mystical co-mingling of minds is false. Richards states that with the naturalistic assumption of the natural isolation and severance of minds, "their experiences at best bring under the most favourable circumstances; merely similar communication, then, takes place when one mind so acts upon its environment that another mind is influenced and in that other mind an experience occurs which is like the experience, in the other mind, and is caused in part by that experience."[36] This is Richards's explanation of what he considers to be the prosaic business of communication.

Richards points out that without a proper understanding of the nature of communication, we approach a poem wrongly and try to define it in a confused manner. Forgetting what communication is we try to define a poem as the poet's experience or our own actual experience of the poem. Sometimes we mean both confusedly together. As Richards correctly judges, this involves the personal judgment and this would imply the existence of as many poems as there are readers. To define the poem as an artist's experience is an improvement, no doubt, but since nobody but the artist has the experience, we must be more cautious and more ingenious in our definition of a poem. "We cannot take any single experience as the poem," says Richards, "we must have a class of more or less similar experiences instead."[37] Richards takes Wordsworth's famous sonnet, "Composed Upon Westminster Bridge" as the model poem to illustrate the nature of poetic experience in his attempt to define a poem. From Richards's point of view, Wordsworth's sonnet on "Westminster Bridge" should mean "not the actual experience which led Wordsworth on a certain morning about a century ago to write what he did, but the class composed of all actual experiences, occasioned by the words, which did not differ within certain limits from that experience. Then anyone who has had one of the experiences composed in the class can be said to have read the poem."[38] A literary logician with a knowledge of psychology may usefully draw up a neat formal definition of a poem stating the permissible ranges of variation in the class composed of the actual experiences of the poem. Richards himself is eminently fitted to take up this task. Because of his professional and expert knowledge of mental and moral philosophy, we may describe Richards as a literary logician with a sound knowledge of psychology. Hence, he is particularly qualified to attempt a definition of a poem from the point of view of a logician and a psychologist.

Though it may seem odd and complicated, Richards claims that by far, the most convenient and, in fact, the only workable way of defining a poem is to describe it as a class of experiences which do not differ in any character from a standard experience. Richards goes on to say that "we may take as the standard experience, the relevant experience of the poet when contemplating the completed composition. In the case of "Kubla Khan", which Coleridge describes merely as a psychological curiosity without poetic merits, we should presumably have to take his dream-experience as our standard." Richards, therefore, concludes his argument with these words, "Anyone whose experience approximates in this degree to the standard experience will be able to judge the poem and his remarks about it will be about some experience included in the class."[39]

It is quite natural for a literary logician with a psychological orientation to deplore the backwardness of critical theory. If, as he notes, the definition of a poem is a matter of so much difficulty and complexity, the discussion of the principles by which poetry should be judged may be expected to be confused.

Richards's definition of a poem has been subjected to severe criticism. In *The Mode of Existence of a Literary Work of Art* (1942), René Wellek is sharply critical of the psychological theory that a poem is the experience of the reader. He attempts a searching and trenchant criticism of Richards's psychological definition of a poem in terms of the experience of the poet. A poem, it is argued, is nothing outside the mental processes of individual readers and is thus identical with the mental state or process which we experience in reading or listening to a poem. René Wellek goes on to say that the psychological theory is only slightly improved by Richards when he defines a poem as "the experience of the right kind of reader." Obviously, Wellek argues that the whole problem is shifted conveniently by Richards to the conception of the right kind of reader. Hence, the meaning of the adjection "right" becomes the important consideration. But even assuming the ideal condition of mood in a reader of the finest background and the best training, the definition remains unsatisfactory. René Wellek points out that Richards's definition of a poem puts the essence of the poem into a momentary experience which even the right kind of reader could not repeat unchanged. It will always fall short of the full meaning of a poem at any given instance and will always add the inevitable personal elements to the reading. René Wellek seeks a clarification from the psychological theorists as to what they mean by the experience of the author. He goes on to say that anytime of his life, after the creation of his work, when he re-reads it, the poet has obviously become simply a reader of his work and is liable to errors and misinterpretations of his own work almost as much as any reader. "Many instances of glaring misinterpretations of his own work by an author could be collected, as in the case of Browning."[40] Wellek comments that "the whole psychological approach through states of mind, whether of the reader or the listener or the speaker or the author raises more problems than it can possibly solve."[41] The conclusion drawn by René Wellek thus sums up the discussion: "A poem...is not an individual experience or a sum of experiences, but only a potential cause of experience." According to him, "Definition in terms of states of mind fails because it cannot account for the normative character of the genuine poem, for the simple fact that it might be experienced correctly or incorrectly. In every individual experience, only a small part can be considered as adequate to the true poem. Thus, the real poem must be conceived as a system of norms, realized only partially in the actual experience of the many readers. Every single experience (reading, writing and so forth) is only an attempt more or less successful and complete to grasp this set of norms or standards."[42]

To my mind, it appears that René Wellek's scathing criticism of Richards's psychological definition of a poem is harsh and vulgar. In fact, Richards says much the same thing as René Wellek when he defines a poem as a class of experiences which do not differ in any substantial form from a standard experience. The truth is that Wellek's conception of the poem as a system of norms, realized only partially in the actual experience of its many readers, corresponds to Richards's conception of the standard experience or the class of experiences similar to that evoked by the poem. It must be noted that Richards's definition of a poem, if carried to its logical conscious, may lead to solipsism. To define a poem in terms of the experience of the reader may imply a negative attitude to the actual poem. It may lead the psychological critic to ignore the reality of the verbal structure erected by the poet.

Richards does not ignore the objective reality of the poem as an artefact. He considers verse to be superior to prose for the most difficult and deepest communications. Poetry is, by far, a more complex vehicle for communication than prose. Communications involving attitudes are deeper than those in which references alone are concerned. Abstract and analytical prose depends for its success upon the shallowness of its thought. It must avoid any stirring of the emotions lest its required distinctions becomes obscured.[43] From Richards's point of view, the poet or the artist has special communicative gifts. He differs from the ordinary person by virtue of the range, delicacy and freedom of the connections he is able to make between different elements of his experience.

The second chapter of *The Principles of Literary Criticism* is suitably entitled as "The Phantom Aesthetic State." In it, Richards registers a vigorous protest against what he expressively describes as the virtual attempt in Kant's *Critique of Judgment to* "Annex aesthetics to Idealism".[44] Metaphysical aesthetics has prevented realistic and objective considerations as to value. It has given rise to what Richards trenchantly, describes as "the phantom problem of the aesthetic mode or aesthetic state."[45] This is a legacy from the day of abstract investigation into the Good, the Beautiful and the True. Richards questions if there is such a thing as the aesthetic state, or any aesthetic character of experiences which is *suigeneris*. The question is whether a certain kind of experience is or not like any other kinds of experience. One experience may differ from another only in degree of likeness. Richards argues, in the light of common sense, that there are all sorts of experience involved in the values of arts and that attributions of Beauty arising from all sorts of causes. Yet the vast majority of post-Kantian writers have contended that the aesthetic experience is peculiar and specific. With due reflection, Richards takes the audacious step of running counter to the tradition of post-Kantian Metaphysical Aesthetics. He argues that art and the rest of human activity are continuous. He notes that the case of distinct aesthetic species of experience may take two forms. It is maintained in some quarters that there is some unique kind of mental element which enters into aesthetic experiences and into no others. Thus, Clive Bell refers to a unique aesthetic emotion as the differentia. But as Richards affirms, psychology has no place for aesthetic emotion. Vernon Lee herself, in her book entitled *The Beautiful*, insists that empathy enters into innumerable other experiences as well as into experiences of beauty. Alternatively, the aesthetic experience may contain no unique constituent. It is commonly supposed to contain the usual stuff but it is supposed to be invested with a special form. The special form is usually described in terms of disinterestedness, detachment, distance and impersonality, and is sometimes no more than a consequence of the form in which communication of the experience takes place. Thus, Richards explains the two senses in which the objective "aesthetic" is used. He tries to clarify the semantic confusions.

Richards maintains that the aesthetic experience has nothing peculiar and specific about it. The aesthetic mode is wrongly supposed to be a peculiar way of regarding things which can be experienced, whether the resulting experiences are valuable, disvaluable or indifferent. Richards is at pains to show that experiences of beauty are closely similar to many other experiences. Aesthetic experiences differ from ordinary experiences chiefly in the connections between their constituents. Richards maintains, "that they are only a further development, a finer organization of ordinary experiences and not in the least a new and different kind of thing."[46] Our experience of looking at a picture or of reading a poem or of listening to music is not something fundamentally different from our ordinary experiences. Richards nails to the ground the false theory of the severance and disconnection between 'aesthetic' and ordinary experience. Clive Bell, thus, makes an extreme statement of the Aesthetic Hypothesis: "To appreciate a work of art we need bring with us nothing from life, no knowledge of its ideas and affairs, no familiarity with its emotions."[47] A.C. Bradley's statement that the nature of the aesthetic experience is to be not a part, nor yet a copy, of the real world, but a world in itself, independent, complete, autonomous, is unacceptable to Richards. Thus, Richards regards poetry as the co-ordination through complex uses of language of the detailed content of our lives.

NOTES

1. I.A. Richards, *The Principles of Literary Criticism*, p. 85.
2. *Ibid.*, p. 88.
3. *Ibid.*, p. 89.
4. *Ibid.*
5. *Ibid.*, p. 90.
6. *Ibid.*
7. Nowell E. Smith ed. "Wordsworth's Literary Critics" (London, 1925) Quoted in David Daiches ed. *Critical Approach to Literature*, (Longman, Green London, New York, p. 93).
8. Lives of the Poets.
9. I.A. Richards, *The Principles of Literary Criticism*, p. 95.

10. *Ibid.*, pp. 96-97.
11. *Ibid.*, p. 97.
12. *Ibid.*
13. *Ibid.*, p. 99.
14. *Ibid.*, p. 107.
15. *Ibid.*, pp. 109-10.
16. *Ibid.*, p. 113.
17. I.A. Richards, *Poetries and Sciences*, p. 93.
18. *Ibid.*, p. 25.
19. *Ibid.*
20. *Ibid.*, p. 26.
21. *Ibid.*, p. 30.
22. I.A. Richards, *Practical Criticism*, p. 180.
23. *Ibid.*
24. Denys Thompson: *Reading and Discrimination* (London, 1955), p. 22.
25. *Ibid.*
26. Jeremy P. Schiller, *I.A. Richards' Theory of Literature* (New Haven, 1969), p. 51.
27. I.A. Richards, *Poetries and Sciences*, p. 32.
28. *Ibid.*, p. 33.
29. *Ibid.*
30. *Ibid.*, p. 34.
31. I.A. Richards, *The Meaning of Meaning*, p. 207.
32. I.A. Richards, *The Principles of Literary Criticism*, p. 175.
33. *Ibid.*, p. 176.
34. *Ibid.*
35. *Ibid.*
36. *Ibid.*, p. 177.
37. *Ibid.*, p. 226.
38. *Ibid.*
39. *Ibid.*, p. 227.
40. René Wellek's "The Mode of Existence of a Work of Art" in Robert Winster Stallman ed: *Critiques and Essays in Criticism* (1920-1928), p. 216.
41. *Ibid.*, p. 218.
42. *Ibid.*
43. I.A. Richards, *The Principles of Literary Criticism*, p. 179.
44. *Ibid.*, p. 12.
45. *Ibid.*
46. *Ibid.*, p. 16.
47. Clive Bell, *Art*, p. 25.

Richards's Theory of Value as Applied to Poetry

5

Richards's criticism of literary or poetic values is derived from his general theory of value. Criticism is conceived by Richards as "the endeavour to discriminate between experiences and to evaluate them."[1] To him, the critic's whole occupation is an application and exercise on the subject of value. The critic cannot possibly avoid using some ideas about value.[2] Richards regards a proper account of value as one of the two important tasks of any theory of criticism, for the critic is not only to discriminate between experience evoked by a work of art but he is also to evaluate them. Richards, therefore, deplores the common avoidance of all discussion of the wider social and moral aspects of the arts. The arts have a fundamental pre-occupation with the problem of social and cultural health. "For the critic," says Richards, "is as closely occupied with the health of the mind as with the health of the body." In this context, Richards defines health as to describe the healthiest mind as "that capable of securing the greatest amount of value."[3]

Criticism to be useful, from Richards's point of view, must formulate a general theory of value and an explicit set of principles. In order to find a defensible position for those who believe that the arts are value, Richards proceeds to formulate a general theory of value which will show the place and function of the arts in the whole system of values.[4] In view of the wide gulf developing between popular taste and trained discrimination with the increase of population, standards are in much more need of defence than they used to be. A well-grounded general theory of value is necessary for criticism to habilitate the critic, to defend accepted standards against Tolstoy's fierce onslaught against all the arts. Tolstoy judges the value-content of the arts by an appeal to the religious consciousness of the age. "For Tolstoy the religious consciousness is the higher comprehension of the meaning of life, and thus, according to him, is the universal union of men with God and with one another."[5] For Tolstoy all human endeavours are without value except those which tend directly to the union of men and promote universal brotherhood. On the basis of this doctrinaire approach, Tolstoy presents a queer, eccentric view of literature and the arts. "All art which does not directly urge the union of men, or whose appeal is suspected to be limited to cultured and aristocratic circles, is condemned."[6] Such great poets as Shakespeare, Dante and Goethe are rejected and denigrated. Such works as *A Tale of Two Cities*, *The Adam Bede*, *Les Miserables* and *Uncle Tom's Cabin* are eulogized. Richards accepts Tolstoy's infection theory of arts in so far as it stresses the importance of communicating one's experiences to others. But he finds Tolstoy guilty of introducing moral pre-occupation in the judgment of values. He is severely critical of the doctrinaire and dogmatic approach of Tolstoy in his "What is Art" to the problem of aesthetic beauty. Though Leo Tolstoy was himself a great moralist, a great artist, it is ironic that his denunciation of all the arts confuses the issue of the moral function of art.

"To protect the arts against the crude moralities of Puritans and perverts,"[7] Richards finds it obligatory to formulate a well-grounded general theory of value, so that a theory of poetic values may be deduced from the general account of valuation. An understanding of the experience of the arts, of what happens in the arts is needed for the theory. The two problems, "what is good?" and "what are the arts?" are inter-connected.

The vision of experience (or mental states or processes) into good and bad and valuable and the reverse, has been generally done without a clear realization of what constitutes "value." It is wrong to believe that the idea of 'good' is unanalysable or that it refers to some special ethical property. The idea of ultimate good is, from Richards's point of view, an unreal abstraction, a premature ultimate. Richards does not accept the viewpoint advocated by G.E. Moore in *Principia Ethica* and *Ethics*, that an experience described as good is endowed with certain ethical property or attribute not to be reduced to any psychological properties or attributes. Richards is unable to accept the concept of good as a 'supersensuous idea.'

Richards pleads for a purely psychological record of values. He proceeds to present a purely psychological explanation of the discriminations between good, bad and indifferent experiences. Richards observes that "critical remarks are merely a branch of psychological remarks."[8] This view is based on the assumption that the method which works for the whole is also good for the part and consequently, the kind of conceptual machinery which describes the working of methods, is the same, with perhaps minor qualifications, as that which describes the workings of a poem. There are to be no awkward logical gaps. To speak of organization, clarity, coherence or their opposites in ourselves and to speak of them in a poem is to say the same sort of things. To a certain extent this is true enough. We do use these words in the same way when we speak of both literature and of ourselves, and this may have been one of the factors that led Richards to regard these statements as being all of a kind. Richards regards statements of fact, statements about ourselves, statements about our feelings and statements about literature, as being all of the same logical type. And this belief is something that is not so much demonstrated as assumed. As Richards points out, "nowadays this assumption would be hard to make. We are more inclined to accept what Stevenson and Richards himself, have helped us to see, that the language of scientific description works in a quite different way for that in which feelings are expressed, and that this has wider implications than Richards then believed."[9] We are also somewhat more wary of thinking that we describe mental happenings in ourselves in the same way as we do observe happenings in the external world. But for Richards, with his strong desire to set up a scientific model for critics, this assumption provided the natural ground for a theory of value in which the excellence of a poem or a work of art is determined through purely psychological tests and measured by purely psychological criteria. Richards's theory of value is consequently a general theory, as concerned with moral value as it is with aesthetics and it is designed to give an account of 'value' in the whole of human experience.

Richards finds a basis for his general theory of value in the study of anthropology. On the basis of vast accumulations of anthropological evidence available, Richards notes that different experiences are perceived to be good or bad and are favoured or condemned as the organization of life and affairs alters. Experiences that are favoured by one are condemned by another. There is a widespread confusion between intrinsic and instrumental values. From the biological point of view, Richards perceives that "the conduct of life is throughout an attempt to organize impulses so that success is obtained for the greater number or mass of them, for the most important and weightiest set."[10] Richards is primarily concerned to find out "the valuable element in experience without smuggling in any peculiar, ethical, non-psychological idea."[11] Those who reject the metaphysical view, define value as capacity for satisfying feeling and desire in various intricate ways. Richards starts with a simple definition. He divides impulses into appetencies and aversions. His emphasis is on the number of appetencies to be satisfied. Apart from consequences, anyone will actually prefer to satisfy a greater number of equal appetencies rather than a less. In terms of the Richardsian psychology "anything is valuable which will satisfy an appetency without involving the frustration of some equal or more important appetency; in other words, the only reason which can be given for not satisfying a desire is that more important desires will thereby be thwarted. Thus morals become purely prudential and ethical codes merely the expression of the most general scheme of expediency to which an individual or a race has attained."[12] Richards himself admits that his view plainly has close connections with utilitarianism. Though Richards derives his psychology ultimately from the evolutionist doctrine, his theory of value is based on his version of prudential and ethical codes and it bears a very close resemblance to utilitarianism of Bentham and Mill. Mill believed in the greatest happiness of the greatest number. According to Mill, the ultimate end is an experience exempt as far as possible from pain, and as rich as possible in enjoyment, both in points of quality and quantity. Curiously enough, Mill's line of thinking is basically similar to that of Richards. Only Richards uses words like 'satisfaction of impulses,' 'frustration of impulses' and 'importance' in place of 'enjoyment', 'pain' and 'quality'.

Richards points out that we do not know enough about the modes of systematization, actual and possible, in that unimaginative organization, the mind, certain experiences are found to be more valuable and important than others in the light of our common observation. We have to achieve a very intricate and very perfect coordination of impulses every moment of our lives. "We only know that a growing order is the principle of mind, that its function is to coordinate, and we can detect that in some of its forms the precedence is different from that in others."[13] In the light of his consideration of the history of civilized man and the creation of order and culture out of chaos, Richards notes that this civilizing process is a gradual one of organization, of the fitting together of the impulses and appetencies that might conflict with each other, of adjusting them to the requirements of living with other human beings. In his evaluation of experiences Richards affirms: "That organization which is least wasteful of human possibilities is, in short, the best."[14] According to him, a well-balanced, well-regulated life, free from conflicts, is good. Those who are paralyzed with their conflicts, are unable to achieve anything valuable; they are forced to live in a muddle; they may be condemned without any appeal to peculiarly ethical standards. Those who have achieved an ordered life are fortunate. "Their free, untrammelled activity gains for them a maximum of varied satisfactions and involves a minimum of suppression and sacrifice."[15]

Richards formulates "a morality free from occultism, absolutes and arbitrariness, a morality which will explain, as no morality has yet explained, the force and value of arts in human affairs."[16] The problem of morality from this point of view, may be identified with the problem of how we are to obtain the greatest possible value from life. It "becomes a problem of organization, both in the individual life and in the adjustment of individual lives to one another, and is delivered from all non-psychological ideas, from absolute goods and immediate convictions, which incidentally help greatly to give unnecessary stiffness and fixity to obsolescent codes."[17] Richards, thus, discovers that. "The most valuable states of mind then are those which involve the widest and most comprehensive co-ordination of activities and the least curtailment, conflict, starvation and restriction. States of mind in general are to be valuable in the degree in which they tend to reduce waste and frustration."[18] In *Poetries and Sciences*, Richards re-affirms that "the fullest, keenest, most active and completest kind of life is to be preferred to a life of proper and complete inertness."[19] Such a life is capable of bringing into play as many as possible of the positive interests. But it is not enough to arouse a multiplicity of interests; the interests must come into play and remain in play with as little conflict among themselves as possible. In this context, Richards cites with approval, the Wordsworthian maxim in "Laodomia"

"The Gods approve

The depth, and not the tumult, of the soul."

Experiences which induce a state of harmony and equilibrium in the mind are valuable. "The Foundation of Aesthetics" contains a significant description of the synaesthetic character of a valuable artistic experience. The organization and systematization of impulses are not primarily an affair of conscious planning or agreement. "We pass as a rule from a chaotic to a better organized state by ways which we know nothing about."[20] Only the rarest individuals have achieved the moral ordering of the impulses, a new order based on conciiiation, not on attempted suppression. But this has sometimes led to the disorganization of the normal social life, as in the case of Blake. But many have achieved this integration for a brief while, for a particular phase of experience, and many have recorded it for these phases. "Of these records," affirms Richards, "poetry consists."[21] Richards goes on to stress the close connections between the fine arts and life. Quite apart from the avowed intentions of the artists, the arts are an appraisal of existence. T.S. Eliot finds fault with Matthew Arnold's dictum that poetry is a criticism of life, for its frigid description of the function of poetry. Richards, however, does not find fault with Arnold's phraseology. In stating that poetry is a criticism of life, Arnold was saying something so obvious that it is constantly overlooked. "The artist is concerned with the record and perpetuation of the experiences which seem to him most worth having."[22] The artist or the poet has experiences of value to record. "He is the point at which the growth of the mind shows itself. His experiences, those at least which give value to his work, represent conciliations of impulses which in most minds are still confused, untrammeled and conflicting. His work is the ordering of what in most minds is disordered."[23] Because of his greater audacity, his failures to bring order out of chaos become more conspicuous than those of common man. Poets are distinguished by their amazing command of words. "Shakespeare's vocabulary," says Richards, "is the richest and most varied that any English poet has ever used."[24] It is not the quality or the number of words at the disposal of the poet that gives him distinction but his sense of how they modify one another, had their separate effects in the mind to combine to fit into the total response. The poet's use of words is governed by his artistic mode of ordering experience. As Richards shrewdly points out, "the motives which shape a poem spring from the rest of the mind. The poet's style is the direct outcome of the way in which his interests are organized. That amazing capacity of his ordering speech is only a part of a more amazing capacity for ordering his experience."[25] Richards distinguishes between spurious or fake poetry and genuine poetry. "Poetry cannot be written by cunning and study, craft and contrivance."[26] Genuine poetry is capable of evoking a response which is as passionate, noble and serene, as the experience of the poet. In the creative moment the poet—the master of speech—is the master of experience itself.

In the present age of scientific and technological advancement and material progress, it is imperative on our part to know why the arts have an important place in life. Richards affirms that the arts are our store-house of recorded values. They spring from and perpetuate hours in the lives of exceptional people, when their control and command of experience is at its highest. The arts provide a record of moments of insight and wisdom in the lives of sensitive and discriminating persons. Richards contends that these constitute the most important judgments we possess as to the values of experience. He regrets that, instead of recognizing that value lies in the minute particulars of response and attitude, we have tried to find it in conformity to abstract prescriptions and general rules of conduct. Art and morality have subtle interconnections. As Richards contends, "since the fine conduct of life springs only from fine ordering of responses far too subtle to be touched by general ethical maxims, it is again on the part of the moralist to neglect art and poetry. The traditional description of the poet as a seer and the artist as a priest reflects a somewhat obscure perception and a dim awareness of the value of the arts. Richards endorses the view of Shelley that poets are the unacknowledged legislators of the world. Though their services are not acknowledged, poets imperceptively give a direction to the trend of thinking in their times. In a subtle fashion, the basis of morality is laid not by preachers but by poets. Bad taste and crude responses are not evils from which other defects follow and eventually lead to the improvement of the personality. Richards finds no excuse for the flows of bad taste and crude responses in an otherwise admirable person. In Richards's estimation, "no life can be excellent in which elementary responses are disorganized and confused."[27] "The arts, if rightly approved, supply the best data available for deciding what experiences are more valuable than others."[28]

In *So Much Nearer* (1968), his last major work, Richards, while discussing the question of 'The Future of Poetry,' refers to the early connections between poetry and prophecy. W.B. Yeats discusses Shelley's "Defence of Poetry" as the profoundest essay on the foundation of poetry in English. As Yeats observes, "In 'A Defence of Poetry', he (Shelley) will have it that the poet and the law-giver hold their station by the right of the same faculty, the one uttering in words and the other in the forms of society his vision of the divine order, the intellectual Beauty.[29] Poets, according to the circumstances of the age and nation in which they appeared, were called in the earliest epoch of the world legislatures or prophets, and a poet essentially comprises and unites both these characters. Shelley makes a climactic claim for the authority of poets in the closing sentence of his "Defence of Poetry" by describing them as the unknowledged legislators of the world and as the trumpet which sings to battle. Poets are, thus, eulogized out of all proportions. We are reminded of T.S. Eliot's warning to the critic, "Honest criticism and sensitive appreciation is directed not upon the poet but upon the poetry."[30] Eliot reiterates the point, "To divert interest from the poet to the poetry is a laudable aim, for it would conduce to a juster estimation of actual poetry, good and bad."[31] In the light of Eliot's interests on poetry rather than on poets, Richards, in *So Much Nearer*, proposes an evaluation of the celebrated Shelleyan dictum. Richards would like to read, not "poets are the unknowledged legislators" but "poets are the unknowledged legislation." This evaluation has the effect of heightening Shelley's claim about poets and poetry. As Richards puts it, "that would take the weight off the poor, brief, human, limited poor and put it on the august, enduring, superhuman artifice of eternity the poet can be the means of bringing into existence. That would hand the legislative function over to a being much better fitted to bear it. An influence that is to help us with how we should and should not choose needs all the authority it can be given."[32]

According to René Wellek, Shelley's "Defence of Poetry" is irrelevant in the present context. He asserts that "it must be obvious today that this kind of defence of poetry defeats its own purpose."[33] Richards disagrees with the pedantic, literal interpretation of the Shelleyan defence of poetry. To serve Yeats and others, from Browning to Hardy and on, as Shelley's "Defence of Poetry" has done, is, surely, much more 'its own purpose' than to be grist to whatever academic mills.

According to Richards, a prophecy connotes two things over which a struggle occurs in the breast of the prophet: (1) What would the prophet like to see happen? (II) What does he really think or fear that will take place? What Richards would like to see happen is a disappearance of all poets. He envisages a return to the anonymity of the Homeric poets or the ballad composers. Richards proposes a reversal of the Platonic ban on poets in the *Republic*. "A wise and painful state would establish machinery making it easy to publish poetry but impossible to be identified as its author."[34] "Such a provision", Richards stipulates, "would save the composer of the poetry much, though, no doubt, there might be poets who would somehow regret such salvation."[35]

Richards affirms in Appendix—A to *Principles of Literary Criticism* that the purpose of his theory of value is just to enable us to compare different experiences in respect of their value. Richards suggests that their value is a quantitative matter. In terms of Richards's theory of value, "the best life is that in which as much as possible of our possible personality is engaged."[36] And of two personalities, Richards finds that one is the better in which there is more which can be engaged without confusion. People of unusually wide and varied possibilities pay for their width in disorder and others pay for their order by narrowness. Richards's theory attempts to provide a system of measurement by which we can compare not only different experiences belonging to the same personality but different personalities. As we do not yet know how to make the measurement required, we have to use the roughest kinds of estimates and very indirect indications. But as Richards's theory of value indicates, we are at least trying to know what would have to be measured if we were to reach precision. And "now to make this comparison is surely a step towards the goal."[37] Richards deplores that whereas the physicist has measurements to work from, the psychologist as yet has none.

Richards rejects the theory of poetry for poetry's sake advocated by A.C. Bradley in his *Oxford Lectures on Poetry*. According to Bradley, the poetic or aesthetic experience is an end in itself, with an intrinsic value of its own. From Bradley's point of view, the nature of poetry is to be not a part, nor yet a copy of the real world (as we commonly understand that phrase) but to be a world by itself, independent, complete, autonomous. The poetic experience is to be judged entirely from within. It may be valued for its ulterior worth. But its ulterior worth neither is nor can directly determine its poetic worth as a satisfying imaginative experience. Richards does not accept Bradley's view that the imaginative experience is judged entirely from within. The value of an imaginative experience is judged in terms of its bearing upon life, in the context of its place in the great structure of human life. Richards admits that sometimes, the intrusion of certain ulterior ends may tend to lower poetic value. But the value of certain kinds of poetry "definitely and directly depends upon the ulterior ends involved." Richards refers in this context to the "Psalms", "Isiaiah", "The New Testament", 'Dante', "The Pilgrim's Progress", "Rabelais", any really universal satire, Swift, Voltaire, Byron, as in these cases the consideration of ulterior ends has been certainly essential to the act of composing. Equally, the consideration of the ulterior ends involved is inevitable to the reader. Richards distinguishes between two kinds of poetry, one to which Bradley's doctrine applies and one to which it does not. He mentions "The Ancient Mariner" and "Heart Leap Well" as cases in which Bradley's doctrine applies. The poems present experiences of a kind in which no ulterior ends/enter in any important degree. By taking Coleridge's moral too seriously, Mrs. Meynell misread the poem. Richards makes the point that as poetry is of more than one kind, that the different kinds are to be judged by different principles, "there is a kind of poetry into the judgement of which ulterior ends directly and essentially enter."[38] There is a kind of poetry, part of which value is directly derivable from the ends with which it is associated, ulterior ends do not enter in any degree in other kinds of poetry and as Richards specifically notes, "there are yet other kinds whose value may be lowered by the intrusion of ends relatively trivial in value."[39]

Richards is severely critical of Bradley's view that the nature of poetry is to be a world by itself, independent, complete, autonomous. He protests resolutely against the severance between poetry and life suggested in theories of pure poetry. Bradley, no doubt, allows an 'underground' connection. But this 'underground connection' is all important. Having exploded the myth of the phantom aesthetic state, Richards asserts that the world of poetry has in no sense any different reality from the rest of the world and it has no special laws and no other-worldly peculiarities. The poetic experience is not fundamentally different from other experiences. While Richards does not accept the doctrine of pure poetry, he concedes and admits that every poem is a strictly limited piece of experience, a piece which breaks up more or less easily if alien elements intrude. "It is more highly and more delicately organized than ordinary experiences of the street or of the hillside. It is fragile."[40] Further, it differs from experiences with a similar value, in that it is communicable. We should try to preserve the poetic experience from contamination from the irruptions of personal particularities. In order to preserve the experience of the poet in its purity as far as possible as it comes to us, we establish a severance by drawing "a boundary between the poem and what is in not the poem in our experience." Richards argues, "This dissociation or severance of the poetic experience, is merely a freeing of it from extraneous ingredients and influences."[41] This is not a case of severance between poetry and life, but in psychological terms, it is a case of severance between different systems of the same activities. Richards inveighs against those who sincerely preach the separation of poetic experience from its place in life and its ulterior worths. "The myth of a 'transmutation' or 'poetization' of experience and that other myth of the 'contemplative' or 'aesthetic' attitude, are in part due to talking about poetry and the 'poetic' instead of thinking about the concrete experiences which are poems."[42]

Though Bradley is an advocate of the doctrine of 'Poetry for Poetry's sake,' in practice he does not insist upon the severance of poetry from life. His salutary practice is a refutation of his principles. To evacuate poetry of all ulterior motive or intentions is to misread it. The wholeness and sanction of the critical judgement involves the total response of the critic to the poem. He cannot read "Prometheus Unbound" adequately while believing that all Shelley's views are moonshine, that 'the perfectibility of man is an undesirable ideal'. Again, a purely aesthetic or poetic approach to the "Sermon on the Mount" without a consideration of its intention or ulterior end, would lead to a gross misreading of the work.

Now let us consider Richards's criterion of literary or poetic value. Richards's theory of value is based on the impulse-structure of experiences. The impulses implicated in experiences may be many and varied or few and alike. According to Richards, impulses may be organized by exclusion and by inclusion, by synthesis and by elimination. He admits that every coherent state of mind depends upon both. But experiences which win stability and order through a narrowing of the response may be contrasted with those which widen it. Certain poems or works of art depend for their strength upon the fully ordered development of comparatively special and limited experiences, with a definite emotion, e.g. Sorrow, Joy, Pride or a definite attitude, Love, Indignation, Admiration, Hope or with a specific mood, Melancholy, Optimism or Longing, may be projected. Such art has its own value and importance in human affairs. Richards mentions Tennyson's "Break, Break, Break", Scott's "Coronach", Landor's "Rose Aylmer", and Shelley's "Love's Philosophy" as poems exploring a definite attitude or a specific mood. But he reminds us that they are not the greatest kind of poetry; we do not expect from them what we find in Keats's "Ode To A Nighingale", in Scott's "Proud Maisie" in "Sir Patrick Spens" by an anonymous writer, or Marvell's "The Definition of Love" or Donne's "Nocturnall Upon Saint Lucie's Day."

These two groups of poems, contrasted by Richards, embody two kinds of experiences structurally. "The difference is not one of subject but of the relations inter se of the several impulses active in the experience."[43] A poem of the first group is built out of an unidirectional set of impulses or impulses which run parallel. A poem of the second group is built out of extraordinarily heterogeneous distinguishable impulses. Richards notes that these experiences are more than heterogeneous, they are opposed. "They are such that in ordinary, non-poetic, non-imaginative experience, one or other set would be suppressed to give as it might appear freer development to the others."[44] According to Richards, poems built out of an unidirectional set of impulses or impulses which run parallel, are more unstable than those poems which are built out of extraordinarily heterogeneous distinguishable impulses. Poems of the first kind "will not bear an ironical contemplation,"[45] says Richards. "The War-Song of Dinas Vawr" has a tinge of irony which "Coronach" does not have; "Love's Philosophy" is lacking in the complexity of *Endymion*. The phrase 'Those Lips, O slippery blisses!' has an ironical complexity which "Love's Philosophy" does not have. Irony, in the Richardsian sense, "consists in the bringing in of the opposite, the complementary impulses; that is why poetry which is exposed to it is not of the highest order, and why irony itself is so constantly a characteristic of poetry which is."[46]

Richards formulates his concept of irony in this context of his investigation into the nature of literary value. Richards's concept of irony is basically similar to W. Schlegel's concept of it. "Irony is a sort of confession interwoven into the representation itself and more or less distinctly expressed of its overcharged one-sidedness in matters of fancy and feeling and by means of which the equipoise is again restored."[47] This kind of irony discovered by Richards in *Principles of Literary Criticism* was to become the basis of the New Critics' concept of irony. The ironic mode of statement in poetry is exalted above the large, simple affirmations traditional to poetry. In a lecture entitled "Pure and Impure Poetry," delivered at Princeton in 1943, Robert Penn Warren summed up a generation of discussion about the importance of irony in poetry.

Richards makes a very valuable contribution to the discussion of aesthetic experience. But as Dr. Gokak pertinently asks "it is not clear on what basis a distinction is sought to be made here between emotions, attitudes and moods." Richards has defined attitudes as tendencies to action and spoken of emotions as signs of attitudes. But he also recognizes that every mental event has in varying degrees, all three characteristics—willing, feeling and knowing. Pride is as much a tendency to action as love. Hope is as much an emotion as Joy. When Richards describes Sorrow as an emotion, Hope as an attitude and Melancholy and Optimism as moods, it is not clear what relation Sorrow bears to Melancholy or Hope to Optimism. It may be legitimately inferred that Optimism is a prolonged state of consciousness, in which Hope is established and entrenched as a past stimulus.[48]

Richards explains that because of our inadequate knowledge of the central nervous system, we are incapable of analysing the opposed impulses from the resolution of which such experiences spring. We can only guess indistinctly that a balance or a reconciliation of impulses sustains two alternating states. The switch-board view of the mind prevents the growth of an adequate conception of the mind.

Richards discovers in the light of the contrast instituted between poems built out of unilateral impulses and those built out of opposed impulses, that the equilibrium of opposed impulses is the ground-plan of the most valuable aesthetic responses. Our response to poems built out of opposed impulses "brings into play far more of our personality than is possible in experiences of a more defined emotion. We cease to be oriented in one definite direction; more facets of the mind are exposed and what is the same thing, more aspects of things are able to affect us."[49] This topic is discussed from a different angle in "The Foundations of Aesthetics."

Richards rates the complexity of the aesthetic responses higher than their simplicity. In Coleridgean terms, "the poet described in ideal perfection, brings the whole soul of man into activity." The disinterestedness of the aesthetic experience is to be explained in terms of the response, not through one narrow channel of interest, but simultaneously and coherently through many. A disinterested mind views things from an objective, impersonal point of view. "A state of mind which is not disinterested is one which sees things only from one stand-point or under one aspect."[50] More aspects of our personality are engaged in our response to most valuable experience of beauty or the experience of great poetry. The greatest kind of poetry demands the total involvement of the personality. The more of our personality is engaged, the better we are able to view things in the proper perspective. "We seem to see 'all round' them, to see them as they really are; we see them apart from any one particular interest which they may have for us."[51] We cannot, of course, afford to loose all our sense of interest. But our attitude becomes more detached as we are not guided by any narrow channel of interest. The impersonality of the aesthetic experience, thus, curiously enough, focuses attention on the complete involvement of our personality. Richards explains the characteristics by which aesthetic experience is defined—impersonality, disinterestedness and detachment—in terms of the natural consequences of the diversity of their components. The ground-plan of valuable aesthetic experience is a balance of opposites. Every emotion that is unable to fulfil itself in isolation in any simple experience tends to bring in allied systems. The experience of great poetry induces a state of composure, for it involves the resolution and reconciliation of opposed impulses. All other states of mind lead to a state of deadlock and irresolution in a welter of vacillating impulses.

Richards refers, in this context, to Wordsworth's pantheistic interpretation of his imaginative experience in "Tintern Abbey" and remarks, "The consciousness which arises in those moments of completed being, lends itself inevitably to transcendental descriptions."[52] Richards treats Wordsworth's description as a model and refers also to Donne's description as of a similar state of heightened awareness, "This extasie doth unperplex." In such a state of mind, we are freed from the bewilderment brought in by our sense of maladjustment. The main stress in Richards's teaching is, thus, on the complexity of experience as a criterion of literary value.

NOTES

1. I.A. Richards, *Principles of Literary Criticism*, p. 2.
2. *Ibid.*, p. 35.
3. *Ibid.*
4. *Ibid.*, p. 36.
5. *Ibid.*, p. 66.
6. *Ibid.*
7. *Ibid.*, p. 37.
8. *Ibid.*, p. 23.
9. William Rights, *Logic and Criticism* (New York), p. 9.
10. I.A. Richards, *op. cit.*, p. 46.
11. *Ibid.*, p. 47.
12. *Ibid.*, p. 48.
13. *Ibid.*, p. 50.
14. *Ibid.*, p. 52.
15. *Ibid.*, p. 53.
16. *Ibid.*, p. 58.
17. *Ibid.*, pp. 58-59.
18. *Ibid.*, p. 59.
19. I.A. Richards, *Poetries and Sciences*, p. 38.

20. I.A. Richards, *Principles of Literary Criticism*, p. 57.
21. I.A. Richards, *Poetries and Sciences*, p. 40.
22. I.A. Richards, *Principles of Literary Criticism*, p. 61.
23. *Ibid.*
24. I.A. Richards, *Poetries and Sciences*, p. 42.
25. *Ibid.*, p. 44.
26. *Ibid.*, p. 45.
27. *Ibid.*, p. 61.
28. I.A. Richards, *Principles of Literary Criticism*, p. 33.
29. W.B. Yeats, *Essays and Introduction* (Macmillan, London, 1961), p. 67.
30. T.S. Eliot, *Selected Prose*, p. 26.
31. *Ibid.*, p. 130.
32. I.A. Richards: *So Much Nearer*, (Harcourt Brace and World, New York, 1968), p. 152.
33. René Wellek, *A History of Modern Criticism* (1790-1950, Vol. II, Yale, 1955), p. 125.
34. *Ibid.*, p. 152.
35. *Ibid.*
36. I.A. Richards, *Principles of Literary Criticism*, p. 288.
37. *Ibid.*, p. 289.
38. *Ibid.*, p. 77.
39. *Ibid.*
40. *Ibid.*, p. 78.
41. *Ibid.*, pp. 78-79.
42. *Ibid.*, p. 79.
43. *Ibid.*, p. 250.
44. *Ibid.*, p. 250.
45. *Ibid.*
46. *Ibid.*
47. Schlegel, *Lectures on Dramatic Art and Literature*, p. 227.
48. V.K. Gokak, *An Integral View of Poetry*, p. 55.
49. *Ibid.*, p. 251.
50. *Ibid.*
51. *Ibid.*, p. 252.
52. *Ibid.*

Poetry as Pseudo-statement: Good Poetry and Bad Poetry

6

In *Science and Poetry (*1926), which was later re-issued as *Poetries and Sciences*, Richards chose to describe much poetry in scientific terms as containing pseudo-statements. He coined a special phrase 'Pseudo-statements' to explain statements of the kind made in poetry. It is evident that the bulk of poetry consists of statements which are not verifiable. "References as they occur in poetry, are rarely susceptible of scientific truth and falsity."[1] It is in this context that Richards in *Science and Poetry* describes poetry as "pseudo-statement." To Richards, statements occurring in poetry are "pseudo" in the sense that their final purpose is not that of reporting how things link up with one another, i.e. conveying information for its own. In *Science and Poetry*, Richards defines a pseudo-statement as "a form of words which is justified entirely by its effect in releasing or organizing our impulses and attitudes: a statement, on the other hand, is justified by its truth, that is, its correspondence in a highly technical sense, with the fact to which it points."[2]

Richards may be described, in his own words, as a "literary logician with a knowledge of psychology."[3] Richards was a Cambridge-bred philosopher turned a literary critic. He kept abreast of new developments in logic. The British empiricists were unanimous in their condemnation of formal logic. They accepted Kant's view that "logic, to all appearances has reached its completion."[4] As Richards perceives the situation, logic might be not merely vivid but reborn. W.E. Johnson's view, as stated in his article on "The Logical Calculas," is that the task of logic is analysis—the breaking down of a system into its constituent basic propositions. Every actual proposition is complex. Nevertheless, we may set up as an ideal the conception of a molecular proposition—what Russell later called an atomic proposition which cannot be analysed into further propositions but only into terms just as a molecule can be further broken into atoms. Richards seems to have been deeply influenced by G. Frege, in whose writings the fundamental problems of a logicised mathematics first clearly emerged. Bertrand Russel drew attention to certain features of Frege's work in the *Principles of Mathematics*. Frege, in his analysis of meaning, is compelled to distinguish between the sense and the reference of a sentence as a whole. He concludes that the thought cannot be the reference of a sentence, but must be its sense. Are we to conclude that a sentence has no reference? If sentences appeared only as constituent in works of art, then, Frege will admit, their reference would be unimportant. 'Odysseus was set ashore at Ithaca while sound asleep' obviously has a sense and it does not matter in the least whether Odysseus and hence the sentence as a whole, has a reference. But, when we are interested in the truth or falsity of a sentence, the situation changes, it is then that we demand a reference.[5] Thus, we are driven, Frege argues, to the conclusion that the truth-value of a sentence constitutes its reference—its reference is either the True or the False. The distinction between 'sense' and 'reference' is one of the two fundamental distinctions which run through Frege's arguments. To my mind, it appears that it is this distinction which develops into Richards's distinction between the two uses of language—the scientific referential and the poetic emotive. Frege's reference to Odysseus's setting ashore at Ithaca anticipates Richards's view that in the poetic emotive use of language, the truth or falsity of reference does not matter. Richards distinguishes between scientific statement and emotive utterance. This is clear from his account of the two uses or functions of language. In a scientific statement, truth or falsity is a verifiable matter in the form of a laboratory test or some other scientific method of measurement and qualification. But the truth or falsity of an emotive utterance is primarily acceptability of some attitude and more remotely is the acceptability of this attitude itself. As Richards elucidates the point, "though it is not the poet's business to make scientific statements, yet poetry has certainly the air of making statements, and important ones, which is one reason why some mathematicians cannot read it."[6] Mathematicians and scientists, in their adherence to facts and abstract symbols, find in the statements made in poetry, a tissue of lies. From the scientific point of view, the poetry is a set of lies, and the poet is a liar. Much poetry is feigning, says Shakespeare in *As You Like It*. Plato banished poets from his ideal Republic as poetry, in his opinion, excites the passions and appeals to the irrational parts of his soul. To my mind, it appears that the Platonic rejection of poetry and poets from his ideal Republic has scientific reasons behind it. Richards contends that the scientific approach to poetry is mistaken. Scientists and mathematicians do not understand the proper nature and function of poetry; their expectations from poetry are mistaken. Richards, in *Science and Poetry* indicates the right approach to poetry considered as the supreme form of the emotive use of language.

To Richards, statements occurring in poetry are "pseudo" in the sense that their final purpose is not that of reporting how things link up with one another, that is conveying information for its own sake. Richards defines a pseudo-statement as "a form of words which is justified by its truth, i.e. by its correspondence, in a highly technical sense, with the fact to which it points."[7]

The term 'pseudo-statement' has negative implications. It may indicate that Richards gives a new place to poetry and imaginative literature in his scheme of values. Aristotle says in his *Poetics* that poetry is a more philosophical and higher thing than history. Richards's description of poetry as containing pseudo-statements may be taken to mean that to Richards, poetry is a much lower thing than science and history as a record of actual happenings. Stanley Edgar Hyman describes the term "pseudo-statement" as implicitly pejorative.[8] To Wimsatt and Beardsley, it appears that for Richards "pseudo-statement is a patronizing term by which he indicated the attractive nullity of poems."[9] A. Hotoph suggests, "Richards would have been better to call them pseudo assertions or indeed to have dropped the word 'pseudo' altogether since by reason of its frequently pejorative connotative thing has led many who were unable to use Richards' contextual guidance, to think he was saying something derogatory about statements in poetry."[10] Kenneth Burke modified Richards's concept of poetry as pseudo-statement. Richards's notion is that scientific statements refer to external objects, whereas pseudo-statements are evocative of attitudes. This idea is undoubtedly the source of Burke's earlier distinction between informative and evocative literature. In the later period, Burke expounds the notion of pseudo-statements with delightful abandon, much further than Richards intended. This has the effect of parodying Richards's *Principles of Literary Criticism* by calling it "a mass of pseudo-statements." In *Poetries and Sciences*, Richards stresses the essential difference between the poetic and the mathematical approach to truth. "The poetic approach evidently limits the framework of possible consequences in which the pseudo-statement is taken. For the scientific approach, this framework is unlimited."[11] A scientific statement is falsified if any of the consequences of the statement conflict with acknowledged fact. It has been suggested by certain schools of logicians that a pseudo-statement should be poetically approached in terms of a supposed universe of discourse, a world of make-belief, of imagination, of recognized fictions common to the poet and his readers. A pseudo-statement which fits into this system of assumptions would be regarded as "poetically true" and one which does not as "poetically false." Richards objects to the natural attempt to treat "poetic truth" on the model of general coherence theories as there is no means of discovering what "the universe of discourse" is on any occasion, and the kind of coherence which must hold within it, supposing it to be discoverable, is not an affair of logical relations. The line quoted from Blake's poem, "The Sick Rose" which occurs in *Songs of Experience*—"O Rose, thou art sick," is a poetic statement, an emotive utterance. It should not be treated as a scientific statement; it is not a referential use of language. Richards rightly contends that in the poetic approach the relative experiences are not logical but they arise through our emotional organization. "The acceptance which a pseudo-statement receives is entirely governed by its effects upon our feelings and attitudes. Logic only comes in, if at all, in subordination as a servant to our emotional response."[12] In fact, poetic truth is so opposed to scientific truth that it is not desirable to use so similar a word to imply the two versions of truth. Richards deplores the malpractice which is unavoidable in the present circumstances. Thus, Richards indicates the fundamental disparity and opposition between pseudo-statements as they occur in poetry and statements as they occur in science. It should be noted that Richards does not use the term "pseudo-statements" in a patronizing or pejorative sense. A pseudo-statement is not necessarily false in any sense. In Richards's words, "it is merely a form of words whose scientific truth or falsity is irrelevant to the purpose in hand."[13]

Richards contends that our daily practical existence is largely guided by countless statements, true or false. These statements constantly excite feelings and truth of attitudes and actions. Richards admits that while true statements are, on the whole, more serviceable to us than false ones, we can never contrive to order our emotions and attitudes by true statements alone.

In *Science and Poetry*, Richards refers to the magical view of the world based on our emotional beliefs, customs, rituals and superstitions. With the advancement of scientific knowledge, this magical view of the world with its belief in the imaginative view of life has collapsed, and with its collapse, civilization is exposed to grave new dangers." Countless pseudo-statements about good, about the universe, about human nature, the relations of mind to mind, about the soul, its rank and destiny-pseudo-statements which are pivotal points in the organization of mind, vital to its well-being, have suddenly become, for sincere, honest and informed mind, impossible to believe as for centuries they have been believed.[14] In the context of the scientific revolution of the present century, the accustomed lucidness of the modes of believing are changed irrevocably, and the knowledge which has displaced them is not of a kind upon which an equally fine organization of the mind can be based.[15] Richards points, in this context, to the strong tendency in some people to the habit of attaching emotional belief only to intellectually certified ideas. This tendency, encouraged by some forms of education, is becoming more common through the increased prestige of science. This poses a serious threat to the provocation of crucial cultural heritage; it would ring the death-knell of poetry. "For those whom it conquers it means 'Good-bye to poetry'." [16] In fact, this attitude would be fatal not only to poetry but to all our finer, more spiritual responses. Richards has a passionate concern for the preservation of poetry and all our finer, more spiritual responses in an age dominated by the cult of scientific materialism. He finds reason to think that poetry has often risen through fusion or confusion between the two forms of belief, the boundary between what is intellectually certified and what is not being much less sharply defined in former centuries and defined in another matter.

A study of the later writings of Richards reveals him to be a passionate lover of poetry in all its forms and modes. He has explored the problem of the emotive use of words throughout his writings. We have seen how in *Science and Poetry*, he chose to describe in scientific terms much poetry as containing 'pseudo-statements.' In the essay entitled "Poetry as an Instrument of Research," he spares no pains to explain and clarify his position. In this essay, Richards returns to his central theme of the use of poetry in this age of science and technology. Minds have often enough been compared to central telephone exchanges. Richards finds it more profitable to compare the formation of a sentence to a commercial merger or even to a military alliance. He says, "it is big words which thus agree to combine their powers—for certain purposes and in view of this and that and the other in the current situation and those and these possibilities—we are very much more likely to underrate them to exaggerate the complexity of the transaction."[17] If the utterance is clinched or frozen, Richards goes on to say, it is given the solidity, fixidity, rigidity of responsible prose and we make the sentence, in short, mean what it says and be ready to take the consequences. But there is an alternative. We may use, in fact, almost all the linguistic resources of prose, without incurring any of these liabilities. Richards recalls the angry reactions that were caused by his calling such sentences, as they occur in poetry, pseudo-statements in *Science and Poetry* (1926). He tried to indicate thereby that they are not statements, though grammatically they seem to state. They are not statements such as the statements which build up science or any fabric of factual discourse. Richards soon found that his description of poetry as "pseudo-statement" created a furore among literary folk. A fierce controversy was generated, and Richards was dubbed as a detractor of poetry. Richards, thus, sarcastically puts the issue: "The most powerful pundits, prelates of the critical world, joined in denouncing me, for what? For saying, as they alleged that such sentences are false sentences, and saying this in a peculiarly mean and underhand way."[18] All Richards's explanation, however, failed to convince the literary pundits and prelates of the critical world that he was not calling poetry names. His critics were convinced that he was denigrating the function of poetry. It appeared to them that Richards was reverting to Plato's view, in the *Republic*, that poets are liars and that poets make false statements. From Plato's point of view, in the *Republic*, poetry is a tissue of lies. But Richards's intention in using the term 'pseudo-statement' to describe the nature of poetry was something different. As I have already stressed the point, Richards was a passionate lover of poetry and at the same time, he was a dispassionate critic of poetry. In *Speculative Instruments*, Richards attempts a defence of his position in a spirit of self-appraisal. This prompts him to comment on the use and behaviour of words in poetry. Richards points out that there is an important use of words very frequently associated with poetry, such as does not freeze the meaning of words but leaves them fluid. As Richards explains, the fluid use of words does not fix an assertorial clip upon them in the way that scientific prose and factual discourse must. It leaves words free to move about and relate themselves in various ways to one another. As Richards elucidates the point, "probably this freedom should be thought of as a matter of degree, but as degree suggests measurement and we are not in sight of measurement here and do not know what we should seek to measure, we can do no more at present than recognize a necessity of vagueness. That is not to say, however, that the meaning in these fluid sentences are vague. They may not be vague. As used in this context, vagueness—precision and rigidity—fluidity are different dimensions. In fluid language a great many very precise meanings may be free to dispose themselves in a multiplicity of diverse ways."[19] Richards relates all his findings about the use of words to his theory of communication. We are reminded of his statement in *Principles of Literary Criticism* that "the two pillars upon which a theory of criticism must rest are an account of value and an account of communication."[20]

Richards is ever mindful of the extreme tenacity and precariousness of the grounds of his remark on the two uses of language in the light of one man's actual experience and his imaginings of the experience of others. "So much critical writing proceeds in so serene a neglect of this immitigable isolation that we are taken in as by an inverse enjoining trick and think that is public which may necessarily be private. But, perhaps, this oblivion of the circumstances of such communications is a favourable condition for their success."[21] Much of critical writing is vitiated by the neglect of the communicative aspect of art. He uses the privilege of a definer to mean by poetry "words so used, that their meanings are free so as to mean by poetry, so as to dispose themselves; to make up together whatever they can."[22] Richards rightly points out that the grand old tradition against the fluid and free use of words dates from Socrates. The ancient Greek philosopher, with his passion for the discovery of truth, tried to pin words to a fixed meaning for the sake of definition. In terms of Richards's description, words in poetry are free to mean as they please and as there is the fluidity of language associated with the emotive use of words, poetry is described, from the scientific point of view, as "pseudo-statement." "Poetry," says Richards, "is that condition in which words, being clear of prose-engagements, are still as yet free to experiment with one another as to which meaning they jointly support. Poetry as an instrument of research contributes to the endless arch inquiry, what are we and what are we trying to become."[23]

Unlike other modern critics, Richards has given a systematic account of badness in poetry. He rightly deplores that the theory of badness in poetry has never received the study which it deserves, partly on account of its difficulty. As critics are much too pre-occupied with the consideration of good poetry, they do not find time to consider the problem of ugliness in aesthetics. Richards seeks to clarify and elucidate the notion of badness in poetry. With this end in view, he carefully distinguishes the communicative aspect of poetry from its value-aspects. Richards proceeds to point out that "sometimes art is bad because communication is defective; the vehicle inoperative; sometimes because the experience communicated is worthless; sometimes for both reasons."[24]

Richards restricts the term 'bad art' to cases, in which genuine communication does, to a considerable extent, take place, but what is communicated is worthless. He describes the other cases involving failures in communication, as defective art. But critics generally call any work bad that produces an experience displeasing to them. Sometimes, though the original experience may have some value, defective communication deprives it of its original value. The experience evoked in the reader should be sufficiently specific.

Richards's distinction in the act of judgment between a critical part and a technical part leads to his description between a 'bad poem' and 'a defective' one. The critical part determines the value of the experience, while the technical part indicates the effectiveness of the object as communication. Since value can be predicated only of experience, and not of objects, only the critical estimate, Richards warns, is a judgment of value. The critic must beware of mistaking any technical deficiencies for detractions from the value of the experience. In a bad poem, the experience itself is worthless. In other words, it does not offer any organization of impulses that is rich enough. In the defective poem, the work fails as communication. He does admit that "a poem may be both bad and defective. But to call a poem defective, is not to offer an evaluation, since value can exist only in the actual experience. And this experience somehow exists and is accessible to us outside the words which embody it in the poem."[25]

By way of illustrating a case of successful communication, Richards points to a sonnet of Ella Wheeler Wilcox on love and friendship. Mrs. Wilcox is a popular poetess and the sonnet cited is a favourable specimen of her work. It reproduces the state of mind of the writer very exactly; it has been much liked by readers probably because of "the soothing effect of aligning the very active Love Friendship groups of impulses with so settled yet rich a group as the Summer-Autumn Simile brings in."[26] Thus, an impression of the reconciliation or appeasement of impulses is created by crude methods. Richards reminds us that though this reconciliation and appeasement is common to much good and to much bad poetry alike, "the value of it depends upon the level of organization at which it takes place, upon whether the reconciled impulses are adequate or inadequate."[27] The Wilcox sonnet evokes conventional stereo-typed responses. These stock conventional attitudes originate from a deliberate organization of attitudes. This is a crude and clumsy substitute for a free direct play of experience, while a bad poem tends to withdraw us from actual experience by means of artificial fixations of attitudes. Richards attributes the failure of much popular verse associated with Mrs. Wilcox to the failure of adjustment of tone. Faults of tone are indicative of a very deep disorder in the personality. The delivery of common-place thoughts or feelings with an air of appropriate to a fresh discovery or revelation, creates suspicion.

In this context, Richards proceeds to draw attention to the effect of bad art upon the community. The artificial fixation of attitudes encouraged by bad art lead to great losses on the level of mental organization. Richards hits hard at the devastating, debilitating effects of bad poetry in particular and of bad art in general, on the intellectual and emotional life of the community. Bad art tends to evoke stock-responses, to encourage artificial fixations of attitudes—"Through them the average adult is worse, not better adjusted to the possibilities of existence than the child. He is even in the most important things functionally unable to face facts: do what he will he is only to face fictions, fictions projected by his stock-responses."[28] Richards accounts for the wide appeal of the best-sellers in all the arts of their deliberate organization of attitudes to cater to the most general levels of attitude-development. While explaining their wide appeal, Richards contends that those who disdain them, are not necessarily snobs. Richards takes the Wilcox sonnet to be a specimen of bad art. His strongest objection to the Wilcox sonnet, or for that matter, to any specimen of badness in poetry, is that "a person who enjoys it, through the very organization of his responses which enables him to enjoy it, is debarred from appreciating many things which, if he could appreciate them, he would prefer."[29]

Richards proceeds to compare the sort of appeasement and integration attained through a sonnet of Wilcox with that attained through a sonnet of Keats. Obviously, Keats's sonnet achieves a richer and higher integration than that of Wilcox's. In Keats's sonnet, the adjustment of appetencies and impulses is of a more comprehensive range and depth than in Wilcox sonnet. In the process of the education of our sensibilities, we move from the level of Wilcox to the level of Keats. There is something of a psychological law, according to which, having attained the higher level of integration, it is impossible to go back to the lower one. But as this law is tied up with the structure of the nervous system, even a good critic might, at a low ebb of neural potency, mistake a sonnet of Wilcox for one of Rossetti or even of Shakespeare.

Richards condemns the indulgence in verse of the type of Wilcox sonnet. Undoubtedly the value of the experience which results from it is small. The value of poetry depends on the nature of the experience communicated by it. In the case of poetry, the responses are so varied, so representative of all the activities of life, that actual universal preference on the part of those who have tried both kinds fairly is the same as superiority in value of the one over the other. Keats, by universal qualified opinion, is a more efficient poet than Wilcox, and that is the same thing as saying that his works are more valuable.

In *Practical Criticism*, Richards carries further afield his thoughts on badness in poetry. The problem crops up in connection with his treatment of irrelevant associations and stock-responses. Richards thinks that the secret of genius is perhaps nothing else than the greater availability of all experience coupled with larger stores of experience to draw upon. As Richards observes, "The man of genius seems to take in more every minute than his duller companion, and what he has received seems to be more readily at his disposal when he needs it. This obvious description of Shakespeare seems to apply in lesser degree to other good poets."[30] Bad poets are less gifted; they are men of less endowment. As he attempts a similar achievement with less experience and with what experience he has less available, he is likely to arrive at merely arbitrary results. He lacks the control of a many-sided, still active, past experience and his momentary tendencies, desires and impulses shape and settle his conclusions for him, and it is more likely to be the attractiveness of the idea, in the light of some particular desire, than its relevance that causes it to be adopted. It might be thought that the test of subsequent experience would lead such a man to abandon or correct the inappropriate ideas and responses he arrives at in his arbitrary fashion. Good poetry owes its value in a large measure to the closeness of its contact with reality and it may thereby become a powerful weapon for breaking up unreal ideas and responses. Bad poetry corrupts the sensibility, for it encourages unreal ideas and responses. Nearly all good poetry is disconcerting, for a moment at least, when we respond to it, for it tends to break up our old, routined stock-responses to experience. Some dear habit has to be abandoned if we are to follow it. The theory of badness in poetry brings in the notion of sentimentality.

'Sentimentality' is one of the most over-worked words in the whole vocabulary of literary criticism. Richards uses the technique of multiple definitions to point to various senses of the word 'sentimental.' First, a person may be said to be sentimental when his emotions are too easily stirred, too light on the trigger. Secondly, a response is sentimental if it is too great for the occasion. People are called sentimental when the flood-gates of their emotions are too easily raised. This, then, gives us a precise, though very general, sense for "sentimental," a qualitative sense. In another sense, "sentimental" is equivalent to 'crude.' A crude emotion, as opposed to a refined emotion, can be set off by all manner of situations whereas a refined emotion is one that can only be aroused by a narrow range of situation. Neither crudeness nor refinement need imply anything of value about the intensity of the emotion, though much popular criticism seems to assume so, do not necessarily imply value. Poems which are very 'moving' may be negligible or bad. It is the quality rather than the intensity which matters.

We look for concreteness and nearness and also for inner logic or coherence in a good poem. Borrowed decorations are almost always irrelevant. Richards finds fault with Swinburne for the bad influence that he has exercised on poetry in the shape of encouraging incoherences. Such incoherences are characteristic of conventional verse; only a very intent concentration of the poet's imaginative faculties can prevent such bad influences. In themselves they may not be destructive, but they are a very useful corroboration if we suspect on other grounds that the central impulse of a poem is weak. By the time these incoherent items have pooled their effects, the response can hardly here be anything but crude and undirected, objectless feeling of pathos that will attach itself to anything that will give it an excuse. Before we can decide whether a poem is or is not sentimental, we must be sure that we know both what the presented situation is and what response is invited. The poet can ward off the danger from sentimentality if he can build these dangerous elements into a whole response which completes and frees them. For what is bad in these sentimental responses is their confinement to one stereo-typed, unrepresentative aspect of the prompting situation.

Richards keeps an open mind on the question of the use of figures of speech in poetry. He warns against the great danger of snobbery. Whenever such questions arise that metaphor is conventional and familiar, need not in itself be sufficient ground for objection. Similarly, if the situation and emotion were ordinary, simple and familiar, that in itself would be no bar to merit, provided the emotions were properly founded on the situation. This is what Eliot means by the use of the term 'objective correlative.' In an essay entitled "Hamlet and His Problems" (1919), Eliot wrote: "The only way of expressing emotion in the form of art is by finding an 'objective correlative;' in other words, a set of objects, a situation, a chain of events which shall be the formula of that particular emotion, such that when the external facts, which must terminate in sensory experience, are given, the emotion is immediately evoked."[31] This notion is perhaps anticipated by Pound's phrase "equations for the human emotions." But there are valid grounds of objection if the borrowed second-hand quality of the expression reflects, not merely neediness or carelessness, but a similar second-hand quality on the thing expressed.

Richards's conception of poetry recalls Coleridge's shrewd observations; "Poetry, even that of the lofties and seemingly, that of the wildest order, had a logic of its own, as severe as that of science and more difficult, because more subtle, more complex and dependent on more and more fugitive causes."[32] Richards is not recommending nearness, correctness and coherence as specific for the avoidance of sentimentality. It is the nature of the presented situation that matters.

Richards warns against the dangers of the application of a crude subject-theory or message theory. The application of such a theory will enable us to conclude quickly and easily whether the poetry is good or bad. So, too, theories that poetry must be 'vivid;' 'simple;' 'musical;' 'stirring;' 'passionate;' 'sensuous;' 'impersonal;' or 'sincere.' In fact, so will any theory that gives us a definite character that we can look for in a poem and decide its presence or absence. As Richards points out, the more thoroughly we work out our account of the differences between good and bad poetry, the more intricate and complex the account becomes. Most critical dramas and preconception as applied to the evaluation of poetry tend to act like primitive superstitions to blur our judgment. The reading of poetry should lead to an act of choice involving the acceptance of good poems and rejection of the bad. Richards is convinced that the distinction between good and bad poetry cannot be made on the basis of dogmatic pre-suppositions and critical pre-conceptions. "But in poetry our feelings (in the large sense which makes them as much currents in our will as objects to introspection) are in the end the whole matter. We cannot substitute for them any poetic-thermometer in the form of any doctrine whatsoever without being betrayed."[33] "The differences between good and bad poetry," Richards goes on to say, "may be indiscernible to direct attention yet patent in their effects upon feeling. The choice of our whole personality may be the only instrument we possess delicate enough to effect the discrimination."[34] When we have the poem in all its minute particulars as intimately and as fully present to our minds as we can contrive, no general description of it but the very experience itself present as a living pulse in our biographies, then our acceptance or rejection of bad poetry should be an instinctive act. Such a choice has to be conducted without the support of any arguments, principles or general rules. All that arguments or principles can do, is to protect us from irrelevances, and disturbing pre-conceptions. They may prevent our using bad arguments, but they cannot supply good ones. As Richards warns us, bad poetry has a seductive appeal for most of us, while good poetry has a secret repugnance. Richards points to deep-seated treacheries within us, which interfere with the right reading of poem. "Mere acquiescent immersion in good poetry can give us, of course, much that is valuable. Acquiescent immersion in bad poetry entails a corresponding penalty."[35] Our daily emotional life supplies the raw materials of poetry and so Richards contends that we cannot avoid the materials of poetry. "If we do not live in consonance with good poetry, we must live in consonance with bad poetry. And, in fact, the idle hours of most lives are filled with reveries that are simply bad private poetry."[36]

Richards's use of the term "stock-responses" has now become current intellectual coin. By "stock-responses," Richards means fixed conventionalised reactions to any given situation. Much reading of even the most original poetry is governed by stock-responses, i.e. by conventionalised responses to the experience recorded in the poem. The intervention of such responses, moreover, in all forms of human activity in business, in personal relationships, in public affairs and in courts of justice will be recognized. Richards believes that the study of poetry may throw light upon their causes, their services, their disadvantages, and on the ways in which they may be overcome.

Stock-responses betray us into seeing in the poem only what our habitual responses let us see. Thereby, the real poem is smothered. In the case of a poem made up of stock-responses, we tend to like it because it demands only a passive attention, without the exercise of any intelligence on our part. Richards notes, however, that stock-responses are much better than no response at all. It is almost impossible on the part of the individual to meet every developing situation. But stock-responses are disadvantageous and even dangerous in the study of poetry because they may obstruct a response more appropriate to the situation. The reader responds to poetry in terms of views and emotions already fully prepared in his mind, so that what happens appears to be more of the reader's doing than the poet's. "The button is pressed, and then the author's work is done, for immediately the record starts playing in quasi (or total) independence of the poem which is supposed to be its origin or instrument."[37] Of the poems included in *Practical Criticism*, by Richards, poems I, IV, VII and IX have a familiarity that is a sign of their facility as stock-responses. What is noticeable about these poems is their extreme impersonality in the form of the echoes of other poets and the absence of any personal individual character either in their movement as verse or in their phrasing. Richards critically observes that "each of them might well have been written by a committee."[38] This characterlessness appears very plainly if we compare them with Donne's Holy Sonnet included in *Practical Criticism*:

> At the round earth's imagined corners blow
> Your trumpets, angels, and arise, arise
> From death, you numberless infinities
> Of souls, and to your scattered bodies go;

Words in Donne's Holy Sonnet have a peculiar personal twist. Such stock poem with stock rhythms and stock ideas are frequently very popular because "They come home to a majority of readers with a minimum of trouble, for no new outlook, no new direction of feeling, is required."[39] Richards concedes that there are stock-responses which are reasonably adequate to their situations and they assist rather than prevent further, more refined development. But one should not forget that inappropriate stock-responses are common and that they are powerful enemies to poetry. According to Richards, the chief cause of inappropriate stereo-typed reactions is withdrawal from experience. Ideas are a beguiling substitute for actual experience in evoking and developing responses. Any very widespread diffusion of ideas and responses tends towards standardization. Meanwhile, Richards warns us that the threat to poetry in this age of standardization must be recognized, for poetry is our chief means by which subtle ideas and responses may be communicated. Richards concludes that the only correction to stock inappropriate responses in all cases must be a closer contact with reality or immediately through other minds which are in close contact. Richards contends that as good poetry owes its value in a large measure to the closeness of its contact with reality, it may thereby become a powerful weapon for breaking unreal ideas and responses and may be used as a means for recognizing ourselves.

Richards is not happy with the tone of the official doctrine of the eighteenth century or the Augustan age that

True wit is nature to advantage dress'd,
What oft was thought, but ne'er so well express'd.

This critical dictum, so firmly entrenched in many minds, interferes with the proper responses to poetry, for it questions the poet's ability to present new and valuable experiences. Many readers are inclined to think that every poem calls up stock-responses. Gray's "Elegy", in particular, is singled out as one which stirs up within us certain universal feeling about life and death. Dr. Johnson confirms the judgment. Richards concedes that the "Elegy" is a far richer poem than the stock-responses seem to suggest. Its extreme familiarity may blind us to its peculiarities of tone and sequence of feeling. Richards points, in this context, to the subtle and finely organized responses evoked by Hardy's poem. Richards comments that "we have only to open Hardy's poems at almost any page to discover that besides 'the stock-responses to churchyard scenery', there are many other possible responses."[40]

To Richards, the secret of poetic genius consists in its greater availability of all experience coupled with larger stores of experience to draw upon. The man of genius seems to have a greater range of experience than his duller companion and he has a greater control over it. This description fits Shakespeare very well and it seems to apply in lesser degree to other good poets.

NOTES

1. I.A. Richards, *Principles of Literary Criticism*, p. 272.
2. I.A. Richards, *Science and Poetry*, p. 60.
3. I.A. Richards, *Principles of Literary Criticism*, p. 226.
4. John Passmore, *A Hundred Years of Philosophy*, London, 1957, p. 123.
5. *Ibid.*, p. 154.
6. I.A. Richards, *Poetries and Sciences*, p. 58.

7. *Ibid.*, p. 60.
8. Stanley Edgar Hyman, *The Armed Visions* (Alfred A. Knopf, New York, 1952), p. 311.
9. Wimsatt and Beardsley, *The Affective Fallacy or Critiques and Essays in Criticism*, 1920, 1948, New York, 1948, p. 40.
10. W.H.A. Hotoph, *Language Thought and Comprehensions* (University of Indiana Press, Bloomington, 1965), p. 52.
11. I.A. Richards, *Poetries and Sciences*, p. 591.
12. *Ibid.*
13. *Ibid.*, p. 60.
14. *Ibid.*, pp. 60-61
15. *Ibid.*, p. 61.
16. I.A. Richards, *Practical Criticism*, p. 278.
17. I.A. Richards, *Speculative Instruments* (Routledge and Kegan Paul, London, 1955), p. 247.
18. *Ibid.*, pp. 147-48.
19. *Ibid.*, pp. 148-49.
20. I.A. Richards, *Principles of Literary Criticism*, p. 25.
21. I.A. Richards, *Speculative Instruments* (Routledge and Kegen Paul, London, 1957), p. 149.
22. *Ibid.*
23. *Ibid.*
24. I.A. Richards, *Principles of Literary Criticism*, p. 199.
25. Murray Krieger, *The New Apologists for Poetry*, pp. 59-60.
26. I.A. Richards, *Principles of Literary Criticism*, p. 201.
27. *Ibid.*, p. 202.
28. *Ibid.*, p. 203.
29. *Ibid.*, p. 204.
30. I.A. Richards, *Practical Criticism*, pp. 249-50.
31. T.S. Eliot, *Selected Essays* (New York, 1932), pp. 124-25.
32. Coleridge, *Biographia Literaria* (J.M. Derek, London, 1947), p. 3.
33. I.A. Richards, *Practical Criticism*, p. 301.
34. *Ibid.*, p. 302.
35. *Ibid.*, p. 305.
36. *Ibid.*, p. 320.
37. *Ibid.*, pp. 15-16.
38. *Ibid.*, p. 244.
39. *Ibid.*, p. 245.
40. *Ibid.*, p. 253.

Problem of Poetry and Beliefs

7

If poetry is the supreme form of the emotive use of language in terms of Richards's description, it has naturally to do something with doctrine or message. All through the ages poetry has been associated with doctrine or message. The Renaissance conception of poetry was that it should combine aesthetic delight with teaching. A poet is considered to be a maker, a creator. At the same time, he has to play the role of an educator. Poetry is not a pure art like music. Like other forms of literature, objective poetry also deals with facts and ideas and can be studied with a view to discovering objective truth. It is possible to examine Pope's works as an example of contemporary belief. *Paradise Lost* may be studied as a manual of theology. Poetry, according to the Renaissance view, should combine instruction with delight. The poet's first aim is not truth but delight. Even when, like Spencer in the *Faerie Queene*, he wishes to instruct, he seeks to do so by delighting. Milton and Wordsworth share a high view of the poet's mission, though the source of Wordsworth's ethical idealism was very different from the Protestant Christian Humanism which led Milton to declare that the poet's abilities 'are of power beside the office of a pulpit, to inbreed and cherish in a great people the seeds of virtue, and public activity, to allay the perturbations of the mind, and set the affections in right tune.' Yet Wordsworth's half-mystic pantheism and Milton's Puritan assimilation of functions of poetry and a preaching produced very similar views of the ultimate purpose of poetry.

Matthew Arnold describes poetry as a criticism of life. This worn-out phrase used by Arnold stresses the interpretative functions of poetry. In fact, all discussions on a moral function of poetry are connected with the vital problem of relationship between poetry and beliefs. It is evident that the bulk of poetry consists of statements which are not verifiable. "References, as they occur in poetry, are rarely susceptible of scientific truth or falsity."[1] It is in this context that Richards in *Science and Poetry* describes poetry as "pseudo-statement." "Only references which are brought into certain highly complex and very special combinations, so as to correspond to the ways in which things actually hang together, can be either true or false, and most references in poetry", Richards adds "are not knit together in this way."[2] They are naturally general or vague. Richards contends that even when references, as they occur in poetry, are frankly false, this is no defect, unless the obviousness of the falsity forces the reader to reaction which are incongruent or disturbing to the poem. Again, the truth of the references, as they occur in poetry, when they are true, is no merit in this connection. In rare cases, the explicit recognition of the truth of a statement, as opposed to the simple acceptance of it, is necessary to the full development of the further responses. While reading Shakespeare, for example, it is the provisional acceptance of the truth of the experience represented that is called for.

Richards shrewdly notes that "poetry affords the clearest examples of this sub-ordination of reference to attitude. It is the supreme form of emotive language."[3] Richards enjoins that the emotions and attitudes resulting from a statement used emotively need not be directed towards anything to which the statement refers. This is clearly stated in dramatic poetry, but much more poetry than is usually supposed is dramatic in structure. As a rule a statement in poetry arouses attitudes much more wide and general in direction than the references of the statement. This fact should be borne in mind while making verbal analysis of poetry.

Most verbal analysis of poetry is, in Richards's opinion, vitiated by failure to distinguish between the emotive utterance about poetry that occur in the bulk of traditional criticism. No one "can read poetry successfully without, consciously or unconsciously, observing the distinction between the two uses of words." Richards holds that confusion between the two activities, on the part of the readers and writers alike, "is primarily responsible for the backwardness of critical studies."[4] It is also responsible for stultifications of human endeavour. Richards claims that this distinction is no more academic activity, for there is hardly a problem outside mathematics which is not complicated by its neglect, and hardly any emotional response which is not crippled by irrelevant intrusions. Richards confidently affirms that "a widespread observance of this distinction would bring about"[5] great revolution in human affairs.

Richards points, in this context, to one form of perversion which is constantly present in critical discussion and is, in fact, responsible for Revelation Doctrines. The poet sometimes feels tempted to base his attitudes upon some reference which is treated as established scientific truths and he, thus, easily comes to invite the destruction of his work. In this context, Richards refers to Wordsworth's doctrine of Pantheism and other doctrines of Inspiration, Idealism and Revelation. Being based on some reference, the attitude takes on an appearance of security and stability and this seems to be justified, and at the same time it is no longer so necessary to sustain the attitude by the more difficult means peculiar to the arts or to pay full attention to form, "but the attitude for the sake of which the belief is introduced is thereby made not more but less stable."[6]

The attitudes, which are produced not by the appropriate means but, as it were by a short-cut, through beliefs, are rarely so healthy, so vigorous and so full of life as the others. Richards notes that "this substitution of an intellectual formula for the poem or work of art is of course, most easily observed in the case of religion, where the temptation is the greatest." In place of a healthy experience resulting from "a direct response to a certain selection of the possibilities of stimulation, we have a highly indirect response made, not to the actual influences of the world upon us, but to a special kind of belief as to some particular sate of affairs."[7] Richards discovers a suppressed conditional cause in all poetry. "If things were such and such then... and so the response develops." The amplitude and the fineness of the response in the best poetry, its sanction and authority depend upon this freedom from actual assertion in all cases in which the belief may be questioned on any ground whatsoever. Poetry owes its power to its freedom from assertion, for assertion involves suppression of vital areas and possibilities of experience. Richards finds no need for the assertion of belief in poetry and notes that "the greatest poets, as poets, though frequently not as critics, refrain from assertion."[8]

But there is a fatal temptation to base the whole response upon a belief as to a matter of fact. Even when the belief is true, Richards warns, the damage done to the whole experience may be great. Speaking of Robert Bridge's anthology *The Spirit of Man*, Richards notes that though the passages gathered together are chosen with unerring taste and discrimination, it is degrading to turn them into a statement of philosophy, for such a process tends to restrict and diminish their value.

Richards proceeds to analyse the ambiguities of the term 'belief.' Few terms in psychology are more troublesome than 'belief,' though this may seem a formidable charge. The sense in which we believe a scientific proposition is not the sense in which we believe emotive utterances, whether they are political—'We will not sheathe the sword,' or critical 'The progress of poetry is immortal' or poetic. He defines scientific belief as readiness to act as though the reference symbolised by the proposition which is believed were true. Emotive belief is very different in the sense in which readiness to act as though some references were true is often involved, but the connections and circumstances in which this narrowness remains are narrowly restricted. Emotive beliefs are entertained only in the special circumstances of the poetic experience. "They are held as conditions for further effects, our attitudes and emotional responses, and not as we hold beliefs in laws of nature, which we expect to find verified on all occasions."[9] Richards goes on to argue in *Practical Criticism* that in the context of the problem of beliefs in poetry, we are concerned very little with logical consequences and almost exclusively with emotional consequences. This involves a close examination of the poetic fiction or assumption theory. Richards finds the word "assumption" unsuitable here, for "ordinarily an assumption is a proposition, an object of thought, entertained intellectually in order to trace its logical consequences as a hypothesis."[10] In the effect of the thought upon our feelings and attitudes, all its importance for poetry lies. We may entertain an assumption in two ways: intellectually in the context of other thoughts ready to support, contradict, establish other logical relations with it and emotionally, in a context of sentiments, feelings, desires and attitudes ready to group themselves around it. The intellectual assumption implies a desire for logical consistency and order and the emotional assumption implies the stand or need for order of the whole outgoing emotional side of the personality, the side that is turned towards action. Richards contends that corresponding to the intellectual and emotional assumptions there are two forms of belief—intellectual and emotional, and similarly two forms of disbelief. Intellectual belief is held logically and is supported by evidence in terms of systems of ideas. "The whole use of intellectual belief is to bring all our ideas into as perfect an ordered system as possible. We disbelieve only because we believe something else that is incompatible, as Spinoza long ago pointed out."[11] Similarly, we only believe because we find it necessary to disbelieve whatever is logically contradictory to our belief. In this intellectual sense, belief or disbelief arises only when the logical context of our ideas is in question. Apart from these logical connections, says Richards, "the idea is neither believed nor disbelieved, nor doubted nor questioned; it is just present. Most of the ideas of the child, of primitive man, of the peasant, of the non-intellectual world and of most poetry are in this happy condition of real intellectual disconnection."[12] The belief as to how any person of a certain character would speak or act, probably or necessarily upon which so much drama seems to depend, are not scientific, but are held only for the sake of their dramatic effect. Richards affirms that "the bulk of the beliefs involved in the arts are of this kind, provisional acceptances, holding only in special circumstances (in the state of mind which is the poem or work of art) acceptances made for the sake of the 'imaginative experience' which they make possible. The difference between these emotive beliefs and scientific beliefs is not one of degree but of kind. As feelings they are very similar, but as attitudes their difference in structure has widespread consequences."[13]

Emotional belief carries strong associations of primitive society. "In primitive man, any idea which opens a ready outlet to emotion or points to a line of action in conformity with custom is quickly believed. We remain much more primitive in this phase of behaviour than in intellectual matters."[14] Richards gives a pragmatic explanation for our emotional faith "Given a need (whether conscious as a desire or not), any idea which can be taken as a step on the way to its fulfilment is accepted, unless some other need equally active at the moment bars it out. This acceptance, this use of the idea to action and what not-is emotional belief. So far as the idea is useful to them it is believed, and the sense of attachment, of adhesion, of conviction, which we feel, and to which we give the name of belief, is the result of this implication of the idea of our activities."[15]

The final impression left by a poem or by music or perhaps more rarely by other forms of arts may naturally be described as belief. This emotion or attitude has to introspection all the characters of a belief. This experience arouses belief-feelings. A reading of *Adonais* leaves us in a strong emotional attitude, which feels like belief, we tend to believe strongly, for the moment, in immortality or survival or in something else capable of being intellectually formulated. But the value of the poem should not be attributed to its power to arouse belief-feelings or to its dependence upon such a scientifically doubtful conclusion.

Richards describes most of our strong and persistent belief as "mixtures of intellectual and emotional belief."[16] A purely intellectual belief need not be strongly held, it may grow weak in the conflict of ideas. A very strong emotional belief may lose its persistent character if the need from which it arises is weakened. Richards calls for a clear-cut distinction between beliefs which are grounded in fact, i.e. are due to reference, and beliefs which are due to other causes and merely attach themselves to such references as will support them. Objectless beliefs should not be treated as ridiculous or as incomplete things. This is a prejudice deriving only from confusion. "Such beliefs," Richards cautions us, "have, of course, no place in science, but in themselves they are often of the utmost value." Such beliefs should not furnish themselves with illicit objects "when they are kept from tampering with the development of reference such emotional attitudes may be, as revelation doctrines in such strange forms maintain, among the most important and valuable effects which arts can produce."[17] Most of the revelations received from poetry and music satisfy only a need of the moment, but these have their own importance. "Though the sense of revelation has faded, we should not suppose that the shaping influence of such experiences must be lost. The mind has found through them a pattern of response which may remain and it is that pattern rather than the revelation which is important."[18]

Evidently, poetry which has been built upon firm and definite beliefs about the world, "The Divine Comedy" or "Paradise lost" or Donne's "Divine Poems" or Shelley's "Prometheus Unbound" or Hardy's "The Dynasts" must appear differently to readers who do and readers who do not hold similar beliefs. But, in fact, all good readers of poetry are left undisturbed by even a direct opposition between their own beliefs and the beliefs of the poet. Richards mentions religious poetry, particularly in this context, because the beliefs there concerned have the widest implications, and are the most seriously entertained of any. But the same problem arises with nearly all poetry, particularly with poetry dealing with mythology such as Blake's manifestoes or involving the treatment of supernatural machinery such as "The Rime of the Ancient Mariner." In fact, every passage of poetry which seems to make a statement or depend upon an assumption involving agreement or disagreement brings to a focus the problem of doctrinal adhesions in poetry. It may be pointed out that these disputable statements so constantly presented to us in poetry, are merely assumptions introduced for poetic purpose. But, as Richards rightly cautions, "as the assumptions grow more plausible, and as the consequences for our view of the world grow important, the matter seems less simple."[19] In the case of Donne's "Holy Sonnet" (at the round Earth's imagined corners) actual belief in certain tenets of Christianity is required for its full and perfect imaginative realisation. "The mere assumption of Donne's theology, as a poetic fiction, may seem insufficient in view of the intensity of the feeling which is supported and conveyed to us by its means."[20] Readers of religious beliefs are tempted to react favourably or unfavourably to the beliefs presented and doctrinal dissent as a very serious obstacle to their reading. Conversely, many readers dissenting intellectually from the beliefs presented may read successfully, seeming to believe emotionally in the doctrine presented.

Great difficulties at once arise if we hold that beyond the mere poetic assumption, a definite state of belief in the particular Christian doctrine of the Resurrection of the Body is called for. In that case, we shall have to suppose that readers holding beliefs incompatible with this particular doctrine cannot read the poem fully or must temporarily abandon their own beliefs and adopt Donne's. Both suppositions seem contrary to the facts. In view of the inadequacy of the poetic 'fiction' or assumption theory, Richards brings in the distinction between two kinds of belief—intellectual and emotional, corresponding to the two uses of language. The facts of Nature determine the order and arrangement of the stable ideas prevailing in our mind. All our ideas to which we can lend intellectual credence must be capable of being reconciled to the general body of current ideas. Obviously, poetry contains countless ideas which have no intellectual justification. Hence, such ideas which cannot have a logical place in the most completely ordered system of ideas we can attain to, arouse emotional disbelief. But, as Richards argues from the pragmatic point of view, "the intellectual disbelief does not imply that emotional belief in the same idea is either impossible or even difficult, much less that it is undesirable. An emotional belief has it own sphere of operation, its only justification from the prudential point of view is its success in meeting our need." An emotional belief is not justified through any logical relations between its idea and other ideas, its desirability or undesirability has nothing to do with its intellectual status, provided it is kept from interfering with the intellectual system. Richards describes poetry as "an extra-ordinarily successful device for preventing these interferences from arising."[21]

Coleridge's shrewd remark that "a willing suspension of disbelief accompanied much poetry," records an important fact, but Coleridge's terminology is found to be imprecise by Richards, for in reading poetry with doctrinal adhesions, "we are neither aware of a disbelief nor voluntarily suspending it in these cases."[22] Poetry, read properly, does not involve the problem of belief or disbelief. "It is better to say," says Richards, "that the question of belief or disbelief, in the intellectual sense, never arises when we are reading well. If unfortunately it does arise, either through the poet's fault or our own, we have for the moment ceased to be reading poetry and have become astronomers or theologians or moralists, persons engaged in quite a different type of activity."[23] The reading of poetry is, thus, not a primarily intellectual activity. But we must guard against a possible misconception. The successful reading of it does necessarily involve the intellectual exploration of the internal coherence of the poem, and the intellectual examination of the relations of its ideas to other ideas of ordinary experience which are emotionally relevant to it. The theological ideas in Donne's "Holy Sonnet" must have stirred his mind both intellectually and emotionally and exercised a powerful influence over its shaping. As Richards argues, "The fact that Donne probably gave both forms of belief to these ideas need not prevent a good reader from giving the fullest emotional belief while withholding intellectual belief."[24] Readers who cannot accord intellectual belief to the particular theological tents may enjoy the poem. The very fact that people from different intellectual positions have been able to agree about the value of doctrinal poems shows that the absence of intellectual belief, need not cripple emotional belief, though evidently enough, in some persons, it may.

Science and Poetry, which contains an extension of the psychological theorizing of "Principles", provides a more acute analysis of the relationship of poetry and beliefs. "The business of the poet is to give order and coherence and so freedom, to body of experience."[25] The poet does this through words used in many varied ways.

Distinguishing between scientific statement and emotive utterance, Richards stresses the essential distinction between the poetic and the mathematical approaches to truth. "The poetic approach evidently limits the framework of possible consequences into which the pseudo-statement is taken. For the scientific approach this framework is limited."[26] A scientific statement is falsified if any of the consequences of the statement conflict with acknowledged fact. Richards contends that in the poetic approach the relevant consequences are not logical. In fact, poetic truth is so opposed to scientific truth that it is not desirable to use so similar a word to imply the two versions of truth.

Richards deplores the practice which is unavoidable in the present circumstances. Our daily practical existence is largely guided by countless statements, true or false. While Richards admits that "true statements are, on the whole, more serviceable to us than false ones, we can never contrive to order our emotions and attitudes by true statements alone. In the context of the scientific revolution of the present century, the accustomed incidences of the modes of believing are changed irrevocably, and the knowledge which has displaced them is not of a kind upon which an equally fine organization of the mind can be based."[27] Richards points, in this context, to the strong tendency in some people to the habit of attaching emotional belief only to intellectually certified ideas. This tendency, encouraged by some forms of education, is becoming more common through the increased prestige of science. This poses a serious threat to the preservation of our rich cultural heritage. It would ring the death-knell of poetry. "For those whom it conquers it means 'Good-bye to poetry'."[28] In fact, this attitude would be fatal not only to poetry but to all our finer, more spiritual responses. Richards has a passionate concern for the preservation of poetry and all our finer, more spiritual responses in an age dominated by the cult of scientific materialism. He finds reason to think that poetry has often risen through fusion (or confusion) between the two forms of belief, the boundary between what is not being much less sharply defined in former centuries and defined in another manner.

The difficulty crops up over all poetry that departs from the most ordinary universal facts of common experience or from the most necessary deductions of scientific theory. Richards cites the instances of Blake's "Sunflower", Wordsworth's "River Duddon" and Shelley's "Cloud". The slightest poetry may present the problem of doctrinal adhesions as clearly, though not so acutely, as the greatest. As the problem is solved without the least difficulty in minor cases, Richards presumes that even in the major instances of philosophic and religious issues the same solution is applicable. But, in such cases, there is a greater temptation to confuse the two forms of belief. Emotional acceptance, divorced from intellectual assent, may create an appearance of incompleteness or insincerity. Richards attributes this mistake to a double meaning of 'belief.' He suggests, as a remedy, a further differentiation of the modes of believing the Hows of believing. As both, intellectual and emotional forms of belief, have distinct functions, emotional assent without intellectual belief does not involve insincerity. As Richards frequently notes, words have a prodigious power over our lives and the two forms of belief wrongly tend to be identified. As scientific knowledge alone cannot meet the needs of our living, Richards suggests a division of the world of knowledge, the 'what' or content of believing into worlds incommensurable in respect of so called degrees of reality. We need no scientific beliefs if we are to read *King Lear* and properly appreciate it. In Richards's view, introduction of inappropriate kinds of believing into poetry is "profanation of poetry."[29]

Richards is severely critical of the persistent attempts in traditional criticism to use poetry as a denial or as a corrective criticism to use poetry as a corrective of science. Even the best minds from pre-historic times until the present have persistently endeavoured to persuade men that the functions of science and poetry are identical or that the one is a "higher form" of the other, or that they conflict and we must choose between the two. Belief in poetic truths will have the effect of transfiguring the world for us and enable us to live finely. Richards describes the transcendental and metaphysical theories of poetry as "various subterfuges to regard poetic truth as figurative, symbolic, or as more immediate, as a truth of intuition transcending common knowledge, or as a higher form of the same truth that science yields."[30] Richards alleges that such theories of poetry are never worked out in detail. "There is no equivalent of Mill's logic expounding any of them. The language in which they are framed is usually a blend of obsolete psychology and emotive exclamations."[31]

The habit of giving to emotive utterances the kind of assent which we give to verified scientific facts has been encouraged by traditional criticism and it is thoroughly entrenched in the human mind. The recognition of the neutrality of nature, by destroying this habit, brings about for most men a divorce from poetry. This has led to a debilitation of a wide range of their responses. Richards describes the situation in figurative terms: "over whole tracts of natural emotional response we are today like a bed of dahlias whose sticks have been removed."[32] Perhaps this effect of emotional starvation is only in its beginnings, and hence, Richards sounds a note of hope: "However, human nature has a prodigious resilience. Love poetry seems to outplay psycho-analysis." Richards contends that our attitudes and impulses, our natural emotional responses, need not be propped up by beliefs in the magical view of the world, "they are being driven back upon their biological justification, made once again sufficient to themselves."[33]

Finely developed individuals cannot live by warmth, food, fighting, drink and sex alone. Man cannot live by bread alone. Sincere, honest, informed and sensitive minds are bound to take note of the tremendous change in the world-picture. Even a considerable poet like D.H. Lawrence may attempt to find relief by reversion to primitive mentality. Richards describes those who are least affected by the change "as being emotionally least removed from the animals."[34] The disease must be diagnosed correctly so that proper remedy may be suggested. It is futile to throw the blame on the alleged "materialism of science." The old dream of a perfect knowledge, which would guarantee perfect life, no longer retains its sanction because of the collapse of the magical or spiritual view of life. "What was thought to be pure knowledge we see now to have been shot through with hope and desire, with fear and wonder, and these intrusive elements indeed gave it all its power to support our lives."[35]

Science gives us the technical know-how. Yet, scientific knowledge has its limitations. We cannot get from science a justification of a relatively lowly kind of life. Richards finds a pragmatic justification for poetry: "The justification or the reverse of any attitude lies, not in the object, but in itself, in its serviceableness to the whole personality, upon its place in the whole system of attitudes, which is the personality, all its worth depends. This is true for the subtle, finely compounded attitude of the civilized individual as for the simple attitudes of the child. In brief, the imaginative life is its own justification."[36]

Richards is dissatisfied with the explanation offered by the Vienna or the Zurich school of psycho-analysis. He pleads for the cultivation of a habit of mind which allows both reference and the development of attitudes their proper independence. It is not easy to attain this habit of mind. In our desperation we are driven to support our attitudes with beliefs as to facts, verified or accepted as scientifically established, and by doing so we weaken our emotional backbone and interfere with the integrity and fullness of our experience. Richards adopts the strategy of the pragmatic philosopher to justify emotional beliefs. The needs of our emotional life have to be fulfilled if we are to adjust ourselves to the changing worldview. Richards argues that the sources of our attitudes should be in experience itself and if by a psychological perversion we try desperately to base our attitudes on scientifically accepted beliefs in order to adjust ourselves to the changing situation, he warns that "we run extreme risks of later disorganization elsewhere."[37] In this context, Richards speaks of the clash of ideas between the hard-headed positivist and the dogmatic followers of religion. The man of science suffers from an insufficient material for the development of his attitudes and the advocate of the traditional religious view of life suffers from an intellectual bondage and unconscious sincerity. The hard-headed positivist—the man of science—starves himself emotionally and the convinced adherent of a religion tries to justify his religious faith artificially by invoking scientific beliefs. Richards stresses the dual necessity of a clear and impartial awareness of "the nature of the world in which we live and the development of attitudes which will enable us to live in it finely."[38] He asserts that neither can be subordinated to the other. Richards reflects his pragmatism in making this recommendation. He refers, in this context, to the effect upon us of those works of art which must unmistakably attune us to existence. "The central experience of tragedy and its chief value is an attitude indispensable for a fully developed life."[39] But in the reading of *King Lear*, facts verifiable by science are not relevant. For the sake of greater clarity, Richards refers to the experience of certain forms of music, architecture and abstract design, in which attitudes are evoked and developed which are unquestionably independent of all beliefs as to fact. Richards cautions against the danger of intermingling of knowledge and belief as a perversion through which both activities suffer degradation. He believes in the clear-cut bifurcation of truth. Objectless beliefs which are in reality merely attitudes, seem to be knowledge. Richards finds a psychological explanation for this: "some system of impulses not ordinarily in adjustment with itself or adjusted to the world finds something which orders it or gives it fit exercise."[40] This accounts for "the peculiar sense of ease, of restfulness, of free unimpeded activity, and the feeling of acceptance, of something more positive than aquiescence."[41] This feeling gives such states the status of beliefs, and makes us "ready for life in some particular phase," with our response intensified. "Such are the occasions upon which the arts seem to lift away the burden of existence, and we seem ourselves to be looking into the heart of things." Richards claims that the experience of great art stimulates us to see things as they are so that we acquire clarity of vision.

Revelation Doctrines do not actually imply knowledge verifiable by science; they suggest the conscious accompaniment of our successful adjustment to life. Bogus revelations, induced by spurious causes such as the taking of a dose of alcohol or artificial methods, should be guarded against. Revelation Doctrines do not reveal knowledge in the scientific sense of the term. They produce what Richards describe as "belief feelings." These belief feelings, being parasitic, attach themselves to all kinds of hosts, but in music and in the non-representative arts, it is not easy to find something to believe in. But the feeling of significance is as common in these other arts as in literature.

Traditionally, the arts are credited with the power of giving us knowledge of Beauty, "a remote and divine entity not otherwise to be apprehended, one of the Eternal Absolute Values."[42] This emotive power of talking is effective for a while. In moments of significance, Beauty, Goodness and Truth are hypostatized, identified and worshipped as the Trinity in Unity and Unity in Trinity. Human speech in such cases presents the temptation to illicit speech. "To excite a serious and reverent attitude is one thing. To set forth an explanation is another". These are the two distinct functions of language. "To confuse the two and mistake the incitement of an attitude for statement of fact is a practice which should be discouraged."[43] Intellectual dishonesty should not be permitted to camouflage itself with emotional sanctities. Men should not feel tempted to sacrifice the integrity of their thought and feeling under the influence of illicit belief.

How seriously are we required to believe the statements we read in poetry, and how definitely must the poet believe what he writes? Is there any essential connection between belief and enjoyment? T.S. Eliot, in his frequent discussions of the problem of poetic belief, agrees with Richards on fundamental principles. Eliot tells us that neither the poet nor the reader is obliged to believe in the ordinary way in the ideas which have been assimilated into the poetry or on which the poetry more or less tacitly rests. As Kristian Smidt observes, "Altogether, there seems to have been a constant sceptical and an analytical tendency in Eliot's early speculations on belief and meaning."[44] Eliot read Dante and found that Dante's ideas, his medieval theology and philosophy, would stand in the way of enjoyment, if they had to be fully believed in. He could not believe in them, but nevertheless recognized the greatness of the poetry. So he not only decided that real belief was unnecessary but even that Dante need not have believed in these things himself. Later, when he was drawn into a discussion with I.A. Richards on the question of poetic belief, he somewhat modified his early views, but they were not fundamentally changed.

Richards agrees with Eliot in thinking that strict belief need not be accorded to the ideas or philosophy employed by a poet. He goes a step further than Eliot in repudiating the rational meaning of poetry. This makes Eliot accuse him of wanting poets to create in a vacumn. According to Richards, "it is never what a poem says which matters, but what it is." The poet is not writing like a scientist. Poetry is produced by and in turn acts on an intricate system of interests in the mind and its worth is a matter of degree to which it moves the mind towards a wider equilibrium. Only scientific knowledge can now command belief in anything in the old sense, but this knowledge is not sufficient for a fine organization of the mind. Scientific knowledge cannot be trusted to give emotional support to our lives to prop us emotionally. The only remedy that suggests itself to Richards is to cut our pseudo-statements free from that kind of belief which is appropriate to verified statements.

In a long note to the second section of his essay on Dante, Eliot states his reactions to the attitude towards poetry and beliefs expressed by Richards. Eliot agrees with Richards that the reader can have full literary or poetic appreciation without sharing the beliefs of the poet. If this were not so, there could be no literature and no criticism. He then recalls his assertion that we can distinguish between Dante's beliefs as a man and his beliefs as a poet and qualifies this by adding that we are forced to believe that there is a particular relation between the two, and the poet means what he says. Then he rejects Richards's description of the 'Waste Land' as a poem in which a certain writer has effected "a complete severance between his poetry and all beliefs" as he finds it incomprehensible. The argument that to understand fully the position of someone who believes, means we ourselves have also to believe, had a force for Eliot which he applied to himself progressively. Eliot deduces a general rule from his own reaction to Shelley's ideas: "when the doctrine, theory, beliefs or 'view of life' presented in a poem is one which the mind of the reader can accept as coherent, mature and founded on the facts of experience, it interposes no obstacle to the reader's enjoyment, whether it be one that he accept or deny, approve or deprecate. When it is one which the reader rejects as childish or feeble, it may, for a reader of well developed mind, set up an almost complete check."[45]

Richards does not find any need for intellectual belief in poetry. Whereas Richards distinguishes between intellectual and emotional belief, Eliot does not reject intellectual belief in poetry but distinguishes instead between what we may call genuine belief and assumed or temporary belief. He repudiates Richards's idea of separating sensibility and intellect and finds his division of belief into two kinds both unnatural and unhistorical. Belief is not just a matter of two distinct categories but of infinite gradations from doubt to assent. Eliot notes that, irrespective of the rise of modern science, belief has been in constant mutation from the beginning of civilization and will continue to change in the future. It is natural that Eliot's thoughts regarding the problem of poetic belief should have been brought to a focus about the time of his entering the Anglican communion. For Eliot, even doubt and uncertainty are merely a variety of belief. He thinks that Christianity will probably continue to modify itself. Eliot's point of view here is psychological rather than dogmatic. Eliot actually fails here to distinguish between belief as personal conviction and belief as impersonal dogma. From this point of view it is natural to regard matters of belief as being in a state of flux determined by individuality and historical climate. Thus, as Kristian Smidt points out, "by what he implies, perhaps, rather than by what he actually says, Eliot relates the psychological nature of belief much more closely than is usual to the nature of the poetic imagination."[46]

Eliot analyses the particular relation between poetry and belief from various angles. First, he refers to the poetic use of philosophical ideas as a kind of game. This is how Donne used his chequered learning, 'a vast jumble of incoherent erudition.' According to Eliot, the game consists in making a kind of pattern of ideas and for this purpose it is evident that borrowed ideas and emotions may serve the poet's turn as well as his own. Since everything is proffered in poetry, the question of sincerity does not arise. Secondly, Eliot points to the emotional rendering of the poet's philosophy which, as in the case of Lucretius or Dante, appears as a fusion between the philosophy and natural feelings. Eliot thinks that poems in which such a fusion has taken place were not designed to persuade the readers to an intellectual assent, but to convey an emotional equivalent for the ideas.

The third possible and legitimate relation between poetry and belief is that of the poetic illustration of philosophy which is already existent and moreover gradually accepted so as to need no rational presentation or justification. In this case it is not so much the poet's belief as the belief in the ethos of the age in which he lives that is exploited poetically. When a poet has expressed successfully a philosophy, we find that it is a philosophy which is already in existence, not one of his own invention. Thus, from Eliot's point of view, the truest philosophy is the best material for the greatest poet. Eliot mentions Dante's ideas on the freedom of the will and the order of the seven deadly sins as things that Dante may have simply borrowed from Aquinas without personally vouching for them. In fact, a philosophical theory which has entered into poetry is established for its truth or falsity in one sense ceases to matter, and its truth in another sense is proved. This is Eliot's version of the Keatsian dictum, 'Beauty is truth, Truth beauty.' The sense in which he thinks that poetry can prove the truth of a philosophy is primarily aesthetic.

Eliot approaches the problem of poetic belief in a balanced and judicious manner. Whatever be the poet's motives for using philosophical ideas, Eliot, while recognizing a wide variety of responses to the poetry, warns us against extremes. It is wrong to think that it is simply the value of the ideas expressed in a poem which gives the value of the poetry or that it is the truth of the poet's view of life by which we ordinarily mean its congruity with our own view that matters. Eliot further finds it wrong to think with Richards that the ideas and beliefs of the poet do not matter at all. His considered view is that a good poet presents a certain ambiguity "At moments," he states in *The Social Function of Poetry*, "I feel that his language is merely the perfect instrument for what he has to say; at other moments, I feel that he is simply making use of, even exploiting his beliefs for the sake of the verbal beauty in which he can express them. He appears to be both inside and outside of his beliefs and interests. Where this doubt about the attitude of the poet cannot arise, one is tempted to suspect the poetry."[47] For Eliot, belief means something that concerns all activities of life at a given time, including both science and poetry. The distinction between intellectual and emotional belief means something that concerns all activities of life at a given time, including both science and poetry. The distinction between intellectual and emotional belief certainly seems rather factitious. One is rather surprised to find that Richards makes the distinction in *Practical Criticism*, since in his *Principles of Literary Criticism,* he insists so strongly on the similarity between aesthetic experience and experiences of any other kind and on the essential oneness of all psychic or neural activity. The actual movement of belief is always an affair of the emotions, as even Richards recognizes when he defines belief as the sense of attachment, of adhesion, of conviction which we feel. Kristian Smidt contends that what Richards calls intellectual belief is really an emotional belief caused by the perception of cohesion, completeness and harmony in ideas.

Eliot and Richards have basically similar approaches to the problem of belief in poetry. While Richards recognizes mainly two kinds of belief, Eliot discusses various grades and degrees of belief. Eliot's main objection is to Richards's distinction between intellectual and emotional belief. Eliot considers the problem of belief in terms of his reading of the philosophy of F.H. Bradley. He conceives the problem of belief more or less on the same lines as F.H. Bradley conceives of thought. Thought in Bradleyan terms is absorbed into a fuller experience which also comprises feeling and will. In his *Note on Poetry and Belief* Eliot holds that belief as a psychological phenomenon varies with the times and individuals and implies that it is a matter of sympathetic understanding, not of mere rational demonstrability. He even includes a wide range of attitudes in the concept of belief than Richards is prepared to do, by classing doubt and uncertainty as varieties of belief, just as the phenomenologists class the non-existent as a variety of reality. Eliot, with his metaphysical, transcendental, idealistic orientation in philosophy, and Richards, with his logical positivist, Benthamite, utilitarian, behaviourist and pragmatic bias naturally differ in points of detail in working out the problem of the relationship between poetry and beliefs. Richards introduced the notion of intellectual belief to defend the claims of imaginative life.

Richards's concept of poetic belief is related to his concept of 'sincerity' and his formulation of the four kinds of meaning in poetry. In *Mencius on the Mind,* Richards, like a pragmatist, tells us that "we must acquire the habit of regarding all thinking, even the most seemingly autonomous, as purposive; and of expecting the form of the thinking to be not independent of the purpose."[48] It leads us to think of all statements as appealing equally to the same kind of belief, that is, emotional belief, but by a great number of different ways. The concept of emotional belief is related to Richards's concept of tone and intention. 'Tone,' with Richards, is one of the ways in which the meaning of a poem is conveyed and it includes the many different devices and clues by which the author reveals his attitude to his subject-matter and to his readers. Clearly tone can be shaded off into almost infinite modifications, which the mind can register correctly but which language can describe only approximately: And the same applies to what Richards calls purpose, or intention which is the general plan and aim of the poet when writing a poem, and the organizing principle of other kinds of meaning (sense, feeling and tone). Thus, Smidt argues that to the spectrum of 'tone' there corresponds a spectrum of belief. To acquire the habit of mind of regarding all thinking as purposive means to modify our belief indefinitely in accordance with the sort of thinking we come up against. Since belief is essentially the same thing in all cases, it means modifying the mental machinery by which belief is operated, so as to make belief more or less permanent, more or less intermittent, and to regulate its strength through all degrees from complete disbelief to intense belief. A good reader knows directly or will know from habit that the poet's judgments or assertions have not been tested and very likely would not stand testing from the point of view of scientific reliability. Therefore, he accepts them in a kind of holiday spirit. That is why poetic belief seems different from other varieties of belief.

From the point of view of absolute idealism, Eliot finds no justification for reference to intellectual belief as opposed to emotional belief. As Kristian Smidt puts it, "the latter expression (emotional belief) is induced something of a pleonasm, since all beliefs, i.e. all value attachments, are ultimately emotional."[49] But I believe that Richards has his own justification for distinguishing between two kinds of belief, intellectual and emotional, for he has to defend the adhesion to the imaginative and spiritual view of life in the context of the scientific and technological revolution of the present age.

NOTES

1. I.A. Richards, *Principles of Literary Criticism*, p. 272.
2. *Ibid.*
3. *Ibid.*, p. 273.
4. *Ibid.*, p. 274.
5. *Ibid.*
6. *Ibid.*, p. 275.
7. *Ibid.*, pp. 275-76.
8. *Ibid.*, p. 276.
9. *Ibid.*, p. 278.
10. I.A. Richards, *Practical Criticism,* p. 273.
11. *Ibid.*, p. 274.
12. *Ibid.*, p. 275.
13. I.A. Richards, *Principles of Literary Criticism,* p. 278.
14. I.A. Richards, *Practical Criticism,* p. 275.
15. *Ibid.*
16. *Ibid.*
17. I.A. Richards, *Principles of Literary Criticism,* p. 280.
18. I.A. Richards, *Practical Criticism,* p. 276.
19. *Ibid.*, p. 272.
20. *Ibid.*, p. 273.
21. *Ibid.*, p. 277.
22. *Ibid.*
23. *Ibid.*
24. *Ibid.*, p. 278.
25. I.A. Richards, *Poetries and Sciences,* p. 57.
26. *Ibid.*, p. 58.
27. *Ibid.*, p. 61.
28. I.A. Richards, *Practical Criticism,* p. 278.
29. I.A. Richards, *Poetries and Sciences*, p. 62.
30. *Ibid.*, p. 63.
31. *Ibid.*
32. *Ibid.*, pp. 63-64.

33. *Ibid.*, p. 64.
34. *Ibid.*, p. 65.
35. *Ibid.*, pp. 65-66.
36. *Ibid.*, p. 66.
37. I.A. Richards, *Principles of Literary Criticism*, p. 282.
38. *Ibid.*
39. *Ibid.*
40. *Ibid.*, p. 283.
41. *Ibid.*
42. *Ibid.*, pp. 285-86.
43. *Ibid.*, pp. 286-87.
44. Kristian Smidt, *Poetry and Belief in the Works of T.S. Eliot,* London, 1961, p. 60.
45. T.S. Eliot, *The Use of Poetry and The Use of Criticism*, p. 96.
46. Kristian Smidt, *op. cit.*, pp. 61-62.
47. Stallman ed: *Criticism and Essays in Criticism*, 1920-1948, p. 109.
48. *Mencius on the Mind,* p. 91.
49. Kristran Smidt, *op. cit.,*, p. 74.

Richards's Theory of Metaphor

8

Metaphor is omnipresent in poetry. The metaphoric expression is an omnipresent principle of poetic mode. Metaphor may be described as a condensed verbal relation in which an idea, image or symbol may, by the presence of one or more of these ideas, images or symbols, be enhanced in vividness, complexity or breadth of implication.

The nature and description of metaphorical terms and of the relations between them have both late been matter for much speculation and disagreement. It is unlikely, therefore, that a more specific definition will at first be acceptable. The metaphorical relation has been variously described as comparison, contrast, analogy, similarity, juxtaposition, tension, collision, fusion. Different views have been held regarding the nature, operation and function of metaphor in poetry. In recent years the view has gathered weight that metaphor is the radical process in which the internal relationship, peculiar to poetry, are achieved. Some critics maintain that metaphor marks off the poetic mode of vision and utterance from the logical or discussion mode. Richards maintains, mainly on anthropological evidence, that all language is metaphorical. The traditional view advanced in the old rhetoric is that metaphor is a figure of speech, or a family of tropes involving two (occasionally far) operative terms. From the traditional point of view, metaphor is used for ornament, liveliness, elucidation, or agreeable mystification.

The view of metaphor as tropical, first merits attention. For this view, Aristotle is taken to be the prime authority, particularly in his statement that "metaphor consists in giving the thing a name that belongs to something else; the transference being either from genus to species, or from species to genus, or from species to species, or on grounds of analogy." Some of these instances of transference have been classed by grammarians not without ingenuity and precision under such names as synecdoche and so on. These terms do not coincide with Aristotle's division. And Aristotle's four-fold classification is found, without significant qualification, at the end of a new Aristotlean pronouncement in 1950.

Grammarians since Cicero and Quintilian, again on Aristotle's authority (though based upon the *Rhetoric* where the discussion is limited to prose), have insisted upon the harmony or congruity of metaphorical elements, and upon a measure of visual clarity. Hence, "mixed metaphor" is traditionally condemned and metaphor is limited to a descriptive or expository function. George Carpwell in *Philosophy of Rhetoric* (1841), writes that in metaphor the sole relation is resemblance. Grammarians, noticing some logical incongruity between the elements in metaphor, have also suggested that metaphor not only transfers and alters meaning but may also pervert it, and this suspicion is preserved in the single definition offered by *Sherper Oxford English Dictionary* in which metaphor is defined as "the figure of speech in which a name or descriptive term is transferred to some object to which it is not properly applicable." *New English Dictionary* describes metaphor as "some object different from, but analogous to, that which it is properly applicable." Philosophers particularly, including Locke, have indulged the suspicion that metaphor is an improper connection of terms. They have generally regarded metaphor as an improper connection of terms. Wiltgenstein, the pioneering thinker of the recent anti-metaphysical trend in philosophy known as logical positivism, has much encouraged this disparaging view of the use of metaphor. Metaphor has been regarded as a decoration but in exact alternation to what honest and forthright consideration would disclose in a literal form. Such a view implies that the use of metaphor is a mark of carelessness, haste or intellectual inchastity. This view may be taken to be true of the false use of metaphor or bad metaphor.

Traditionally, metaphor has been represented as a trope of transference in which an unknown or imperfectly known object is clarified, defined, described in terms of the known, e.g. (i) love is a singing bird or love makes you feel like (or as though you were listening to) a singing bird and (ii) My love is begotten by despair upon impossibility. My love is conceived as though its father were despair. These examples happen to be "good metaphors." The only objection would be to the method of exposition. The prosaic metaphor concentrates upon describing, clarifying, delineating, comparing subject to the limitations of plausibility or of logical harmony. Essential metaphor deals in or is seen as dealing in a more complex, instantaneous, and even non-logical relation.

Historically, however, the view of metaphor as primarily a figure for extending description, comparison and exposition reflects literary usage rather than critical obtruseness. Rosamend Tun in *Elizabethan and Metaphysical Images,* for example, has pointed to the sixteenth century emphasis, in hand books and in practice, representing the delight roused by deft and sustained translation; the exploration by metaphysical means of minute similarities guided by a clear notion of the didactic and explicatory function they wished metaphor to serve. Writers of that period saw no reason to extend or explore the outer reaches of metaphor. Although, at practically all periods, we find instances of metaphor serving important poetic functions outside the scope of the received grammatical function. Even the extended range of metaphor used by say, Shakespeare, Milton and Dante, happened not to be matched by any extension in analysis or theory. Johnson may be regarded as representative of his age, but his conception of metaphor was traditional. He looked back at least two centuries when he said "As to metaphorical expressions that is a great excellence in style, when it is used with propriety, for it gives you two ideas for one."

In fact, Aristotle's definition of metaphor, though fragmentary, was far more comprehensive than his successors had reason clearly to recognize. He had also said that "the greatest thing by far is to be a master of metaphor. The making of metaphor is a unique gift. It is the one thing that cannot be learnt from others and it is also a sign of genius, since a good metaphor implies an intuitive perception of the similarity in dissimilars. From metaphor we can best get hold of something fresh or new. Liveliness (energy) is specially conveyed by metaphor."

Richards does not find a finality about Aristotle's view on metaphor. According to Aristotle, the making of metaphors is a mark of original genius, for it implies an eye for resemblances, an intuitive perception of the similarity in dissimilars. The statement of Aristotle, made so long ago, seems final still. Richards formulates a developed metaphor of metaphor in light of his examinations of the fundamental problem. He notes the evil presence of three assumptions in Aristotle's description, which has prevented the formulation of a developed theory of metaphor. He refuses the first assumption that an eye for resemblances is an exceptional gift. "We all live, and speak only through an eye for resemblances. Without it we should perish only early. Perceiving and naming and thinking are all processes of sorting and classification based on resemblance. Some may have better eye for resemblances than others, but the difference between them are in degree only and may be reviewed by the right kinds of teaching and study."[1] The second assumption that the command of metaphor alone cannot be imparted to another, is not found to be valid in the light of experience. Richards, all the time, makes an appeal to experience. As individuals we gain our command of metaphor from others with and through the language we learn. Richards goes on to challenge the third and worst assumption that metaphor is something special and exceptional in the use of language. Metaphor, according to Richards, is not a deviation from the normal mode of the working of language. Richards deplores that throughout the history of Rhetoric, metaphor has been treated as a sort of happy extra-trick with words, as a grace or ornament or added power of language, not its constitutive form. He echoes Shelley's exceptional utterance that language is vitally metaphorical. It marks before unapprehended relations of things and perpetuates their apprehension, until words, which represent them become, through time, signs for portions or classes of thought instead of pictures of integral thought. If no new poets should arise to create afresh the associations which have been thus disorganized, language will be dead to all the noble purposes of human intercourse. The implications of Shelley's words have not yet been realized by rhetoricians.

Richards regrets that philosophers as a whole have not done anything substantial to present a developed theory of metaphor. But philosophers of language have long thought that we can find no word or description for any of the intellectual operations which, if its history is known, is not seen to have taken metaphor, from a description of some physical happening.[2] Jeremy Bentham, a worthy successor to Bacon and Hobbes, points that the mind and its doings are fictions. In this sense, all language is figurative or fiction is the simplest case in which language can be employed becomes a necessary resource. Richards finds a support for his theory of metaphor in Jeremy Bentham's theory fictions. If resemblance is the essence of all meanings, all meanings are metaphorical. Richards starts with a recognition of the difference between the ordinary meaning and the metaphorical in *The Meaning of Meaning*. But he gradually comes to give too wide a meaning to metaphor. In *The Meaning of Meaning*, he states that whenever a word is taken outside the universe of discourse for which it has been defined, it becomes a metaphor. By stressing the similarities between references and eliminating their differences, we develop references of greater and greater abstractness and in the words of Ogden and Richards, "metaphor, the primitive symbolization of abstraction, becomes possible." Metaphor, in the most general sense, is the use of one reference to a group of things between which a given relation holds, for the purpose of facilitating the discriminations of an analogous relation in another group. "In the understanding of metaphorical language, one reference borrows part of the context of another in an abstract form."[3] The authors refer to the two ways in which one reference may become appropriate part of the context of another. Thus, a reference to man may be joined with a reference to sea, the result being a reference to sea-men. No metaphor is involved in this case of ordinary meaning.

Richards refers to Hamlet's soliloquy beginning with the words "to be or not to be that is the question." Should one face the trials and tribulations of life in one's existential predicament?

The relevant part of Hamlet's soliloquy reads thus:

> "To be, or not to be: that is the question
> whether 'tis nobler in the mind to suffer
> The slings and arrows of outrageous fortune,
> Or to take arms against a sea of troubles,
> And by opposing end them."

(Act III, Sc. i), ll. 56-60

When Hamlet takes arms against a sea of troubles, that part of the context of the reference to sea which is continued with the other reference, appears in an abstract form, i.e. the relevant characters of the sea will not include attention by the moon or being the resort of fishes. The poetic value of the metaphor depends, in this case, chiefly on the way in which the ceaseless recurrence of the waves accentuates the sense of hopelessness. This example leads to the generalization that the use of metaphor involves the same kind of context as abstract thought.

The metaphorical aspects of the greater part of language and the case with which any word may be used metaphorically, further indicate that the degree to which, especially for educated persons, words have gained context, with small and concrete vocabularies, employ symbol situation of simple type, which are adequate for simple referents or aggregates of simple referents. In *Principles of Literary Criticism* (chapter xxxi), Richards discusses other forms of metaphor. The word 'imagination' frequently implies the use of figurative language. People who naturally employ metaphor and simile, specially when it is of an unusual kind, are said to have imagination. Metaphor and simile have a great variety of functions in speech. In its most common scientific or prose use, a metaphor may be illustration, providing a concrete instance of a relation which would otherwise have to be stated in abstract terms. Such use is rare in emotive language and in poetry. Shelley's life is "a Dome of many-coloured glass" is cited as a rare example. More usually, the elucidation is only the secondary purpose of the metaphor or of a grown pretence. The metaphor is used primarily to express some attitude of the speaker to his subject or to his audience. Richards discusses metaphor as "a semi-surreptitious method by which a greater variety of elements can be wrought into the fabric of the experience." But "what is essential often seems to be done as it were inadvertently, to be a by-product, an accidental concomitant."[4]

In *The Philosophy of Rhetoric*, Richards treats metaphor as "the omnipresent principle of language." According to Richards, metaphor is always present in speech. Ordinary fluid discourse cannot proceed without a metaphor. Even in the rigid language of settled sciences, the use of metaphor cannot be eliminated or prevented with great difficulty. Richards holds with Bradley that our pretence to do without metaphor is never more than a bluff waiting to be called. A word is normally a substitute for not one discrete past impression but a combination of general aspects. Metaphor, in its simplest formulation, involves two thoughts of different things active together and supported by a single word or phrase whose meaning is a resultant of their interaction.

Dr. Johnson characterizes metaphorical expressions as a great excellence in style, when it is used with propriety, for it gives us two ideas for one, he is keeping to the traditional view of metaphor. A close inspection of the principle of metaphor reveals to Richards that there is an immense variety in the modes of interaction between co-present thoughts. The skill in distinguishing between these modes of interaction has varied from age to age. The Elizabethans showed a wide skill in the use of metaphor in interpretation. This made Shakespeare possible. The eighteenth century, with its conservative outlook, narrowed and limited its skill down to certain modes only. The Romantic Revolt in the early nineteenth century showed a reaction against these modes resulting in a specialization in other modes. In the later nineteenth century and in the present age, there are tendencies towards a recovery from these specializations. Richards suggests a reformulation of the classic. Romantic antithesis, in terms of a better developed theory of metaphor, limited the application of the term 'metaphor' to a few of its modes. It described metaphor as a verbal matter, a shifting and displacement of words, whereas Richards fundamentally describes it as "a borrowing between and intercourse of thoughts, a transaction between contexts."[5] Richards contends that the thought-process itself is metaphoric, as it proceeds by comparison. The metaphor of language is derived from the essential nature of the process of thinking. A study of the working of language involves an awareness of how thought and feeling and all the other modes of the mind's activity proceed. This, again, has a wider relevance to human needs. A study of language transaction teaches us how we are to learn to live. A command of metaphor, affirms Richards, is a command of life. Inspite of various objections, a command of metaphor must be imparted to others. Richards claims that this theory of metaphor has its roots in practice and it must also have its fruit in improved skill.

The later part of *The Principles of Rhetoric* is a survey of metaphor. Richards's first step is to introduce two technical terms to assist us in distinguishing from one another, what Dr. Johnson called the two ideas that any metaphor, at its simplest, gives us. He finds it really unfortunate that we should be entirely without agreed distinguishing terms to distinguish these two halves of a metaphor. The whole task is to compare and analyse the different relations which, in different cases, these two members of a metaphor hold to one another. We use the word 'metaphor' for the whole double unit and to use it sometimes for one of the two components in isolation from the other, is injudicious. Richards holds that with such slippery and vague terms as these, the detailed analysis of metaphor is found to be self-defeating and stultifying. As G.E. Moore has noted, the use of the same form of verbal expression to convey different meanings is a defect of language. To remedy it, Richards takes the valuable step of using the technical terms "tenor" for the thing to be discussed, or the underlying idea or principal subject, and 'vehicle' for the thing to which it is compared or as which it is named. The words 'figure' and 'image' being in the evil assumption that a figure of speech, an image, or imaginative comparison, must have something to do with the presence of image.

Richards is critical of the eighteenth century assumptions, implicit in Lord Kames's *Elements of Criticism*, that figures are a mere embellishment or added beauty and that the plain meaning, the tenor, is what alone really matters. It is something that, regardless of the figure, might be gathered by the patient reader. Richards emerges as a modern theorist of metaphor. He points out that in many of the most important uses of metaphor the co-presence of the vehicle and tenor results in an enriched meaning to be clearly distinguished from the tenor. "With different metaphors the relative importance of the contributions of vehicle and tenor in co-operation give a meaning of more varied powers than can be ascribed to either."[6] While at one extreme, the vehicle may become almost a mere decoration or colouring of the tenor, at the other extreme, the term may become almost a mere excuse for the introduction of the vehicle, and so no longer is the principal subject. The degree to which the tenor is imagined to be that very thing which it only resembles also varies immensely.

As a student of poetics, Richards was dissatisfied with the traditional account of metaphor because it was presented by rhetoricians in a too exclusively grammatical and rhetorical manner. As we have already seen, he coined a pair of terms 'tenor' and 'vehicle' to improve upon the old theory of metaphor. He introduced the notion of "abandoning between and intercourse of thoughts." Since any metaphor, at its simplest, gives us two ideas, he used 'tenor' to mean purport or general difference of thought regarding the subject of the metaphor. Further, he used 'vehicle' to mean that which serves to carry or embody the 'tenor' as the analogy brought to the subject. Richards was by no means the first modern author to analyse the fundamental duality of metaphor. Previous writers had already distinguished between "major term" and "picture" and so on. Yet Richards's coinage and use of these terms to stress the fundamental duality of the metaphoric process has a great significance. His distinction and the term he introduced have gained wide currency among modern critics.

Having traced out 'tenor' and 'vehicle' as the essential ingredients of metaphor, Richards and the critics who followed him, Cleanth Brooks and J.C. Ransom among others, went on to distinguish between the poetic metaphor and other kinds. In attempting to show that the truly poetic metaphor is never merely decorative or logical or explanatory or illustrative, he claimed that the 'transaction' which it sets up between "tenor" and "vehicle" results in a meaning which is not attainable without their interaction. This is to be clearly distinguished from the tenor.

The vehicle brings with it, by virtue of its being an aspect of human experience outside of or different from the experience portrayed in a poem, a host of implicit associations. Although these implicit associations are circumscribed by the tenor these are never quite shut out entirely. Richards rightly ascribed the peculiar powers of the poetic metaphor to the way in which the vehicle, by its mode of comparison, brings with it implicit associations. This unsuppressible range of associations closely resembles what John Crowe Ransom has called "incoherent texture," which he and many other New Critics value as the very essence of the poetic art itself. The assumptions behind Richards's theory of metaphor reveal a new approach to poetry which looks for its lives of differentiation in the special qualities of poetic language, richness, ambiguity, irony, paradox, etc. Such an approach to poetry locates the cause of these qualities chiefly in the tension set up in a poetic figure between the tenor and the emotional, sensory or conceptual overtones brought into the poem by the vehicle. Richards's line of approach can frequently go beyond simply ascribing emotional and imaginative powers to metaphor and claim for it a special kind of cognitive power as well.

According to Richards, the favourite old distinction between dead and living metaphor needs a drastic re-examination. If mounting metaphor upon metaphor were taken to be a stylistic blemish, Shakespeare would be found to be the faultiest writer who ever held a pen. Richards contends that "the best part of the traditional discussion of metaphor is hardly more than a set of cautionary hints to over-enthusiastic school boys, hints masquerading a fundamental theory of language."[7] Not to speak of Lord Kames, all the chief eighteenth century Rhetoricians, including Marboddoe, Harris, Withers and Campbell, and even such a critic as Dr. Johnson are exceptionally limited in their treatment of metaphor. Johnson is abnormally abstruse in his discussion of Donne's and Cowley's use of metaphor. In Coleridge's thought, we get a mature awareness of these chief problems of language. But after Coleridge, as Richards deplores, Lord Kames's *Elements of Criticism* at least pinpointed attention on these problems.

I.A. Richards has rendered a valuable service to criticism by demonstrating the rich and complex variety of the thought-relationship, of which metaphor is capable. Richards quotes *Hamlet*, "what should such fellows as I do crawling between earth and heaven?" In support of his contention that disparities are as much operative in metaphor as are likeness, he cites also the Brobdingnagian King's description of the Europeans in *Gulliver's Travels* as "the most pernicious race of little odious vermin that nature ever suffered to crawl upon the face of the earth." The words "crawling" and "crawl" are metaphoric as these refer unmistakably to other things that crawl, to the motions of fowl insects or vermin. Hamlet, or man and his ways, are the tenor, and the reference to crawling things is the vehicle. The point of the implied comparison to insects of vermin is that man should not so crawl. The force of Hamlet's use of "crawling" comes not only from whatever resemblances to vermin it brings in but at least equally from the differences that resist and counted the influence of their resemblances. But, as Empson reminds us, here we get a Disparity Action, because we have first made a party.[8]

The disparities between two objects are of significance only when we have been impelled to bring them together by an anterior perception of their resemblances. Richards makes the point that the disparities between man and his ways and the idea of his crawling are only secondary, they operate only after the primary resemblance has been established.

Richards refers to another case of Disparity Action from Shakespearean tragedy. With reference to Othello's self-observation "Steep'd me in poverty to the very lips," Lord Kames observes that poverty is here conceived to be a fluid which it resembles not in any manner; hence the resemblance is too faint to be agreeable. The notion of overfilling seems opposite to that of poverty. Richards shrewdly observes that a supply of water is continuously impressed through Othello's relevant speech as an over-riding metaphor, because Othello is losing his fountain or being swept away in a storm. The clash of the general and particular metaphor points to Othello's momentary deranged mind, which is obsessed with images, regardless of their appropriateness. Richards presents a brilliant analysis of this rich and curious Shakespearean use of metaphor, but this metaphor, too, works by similarity.

Richards rightly points out that that is what he calls metaphor. We sometimes get the main stress on the tenor, sometimes on the vehicle, sometimes on the whole combination. Dr. Johnson praises the following lines of Denham on the Thames:

> "O could I flow like thee, and make my stream
> My great exemplar as it is my theme:
> Though deep, yet clear, though gentle, yet not dull,
> Strong without rage, without overflowing full."

Dr. Johnson commends Denham's composition because the particulars of resemblance are so perspicuously collected. Richards finds in these lines a rich and curious example of verbal interanimation and interaction. Some of the adjectives apply more naturally to a calm river, some to a balanced mind, and as they alternate, we are held swaying between the two equally important topics until they seem imaginably connected, each able to interpret and sustain the other. Empson strongly denies that it is a case of metaphor at all. Empson contends that it is a case of mutual comparison that works in a quite different way from metaphor, and notes that if it went on for longer, anybody would recognize it as Allegory.[9]

In eighteenth century writings, comparison as a stressing of likeness is taken to be the whole mode of metaphor. Richards points to the contemporary fashionable aberration in the opposed conception of comparison as a mere putting together of two things to see what will happen. Thus, Andre Breton, the leader of the French Super-Realists, holds that the highest task to which poetry can aspire is to compare two objects, as remote from one another in character as possible, or to put them together by any other method in a sudden and striking fashion. Like Max Eastman in *The Literary Mind,* Breton insists that metaphor works by attempting impracticable identifications. This comes from a crude conception of the mode of action of metaphor. T.E. Hulme thinks that plain speech is essentially inaccurate and that it is only by new metaphor that it can be made precise. This view is similar to Shelley's. Richards, however, does not agree with Hulme's insistence on the importance of the visual quality of the poetic image. Hulme holds that the poetic image should always be visual, accurate, precise and definite. This view is patently false. Poetry cannot always make us continuously see a visual thing or prevent us from gliding through an abstract process. Hulme holds that "the language of the greatest poetry is frequently abstract in the extreme and its aim is precisely to send us gliding through an abstract process."[10] Richards affirms that Hulme's use of the word "see," as an exponent of Imagist Poetry, as just a stimulus to visualization, is narrow and his theory of metaphor is based on a gross misconception of language. According to Hulme, "plain speech is essentially inaccurate and it is only by metaphors that it can be made precise." Hulme further clarifies that when the analogy has not enough conception with the thing described to be quite parallel with it, when it overlays the thing it describes and there is certain excess, it is inferior. But when the whole of the analogy is necessary to get out the exact curve of the feeling or thing that the poet wants to express, we have the highest verse and the best instance of metaphor. Richards finds fault with Hulme's conception of the metaphoric process in his observations: "Hulme seems not to be distinguishing these two examples ('tenor' and 'vehicle') and it is fatal to confuse them as it would be in Chemistry to mistake the order of the complexity of a molecule and an electron, or, in algebra to ignore the brackets."[11] T.E. Hulme strongly advocates the use of metaphor in poetry to do justice to the largeness and complexity of experience. Hulme's prescription for poetry is stated thus:

> "Never, never, never a simple statement. It has no effect. One must always have analogies, which make another world."[12]

But, Richards cautiously qualifies the statement.

> "For one thing, there is no whole to any analogy;

we use as much of it as we need, and if we tactlessly take any analogy too far, we break it down."[13]

As Richards Harter Fogle observes in *The Imagery of Keats and Shelley,* "The principle of poetic imagery, was not in the sensuous, which is a part of the poetic experience, but in comparison, which subsumes the whole of the poetic experience."[14] Richards affirms that language, well used, is a completion, and does what the intuitions of sensation by themselves cannot do. Richards describes words as "the meeting points at which regions of experience which can never combine in sensation or intuition come together."[15] The method seeks to order itself by means of comparisons which bring together objects, concepts or states of mind from different planes of consciousness. In its primitive uses, language functions as a line in concerted human activity as a piece of human behaviour, it is a mode of action and not an instrument of reflection. But in its developed literary and scientific functions, language "is no mere signalling system. It is the instrument of all our distinctively human development of everything in which we go beyond the other animals."[16] Richards contends that to present language as working only through the sensations it reinstates is to misunderstand the developed function of language. "It overlooks what is important in Mallarme's dictum that the poet does not write with thoughts (with ideas or sensations or beliefs or desires, feelings, we may add) but with words."[17] Coleridge compared the growth of the meaning of words to the growth of plants and in studying the law of the meaning of words, he endeavoured to destroy the old antithesis of words and thoughts thereby elevating as it were, words as things and living things too. As Ezra Pound said, "Great literature is language charged with meaning."[18] If metaphor is to be studied profitably, we should be able to understand the law of the growth of the meaning of words. Hulme and the school teachers have erred in assuming that language is just a stimulus to visualization. They think that the image fills in the meaning of words. But, as Richards cautions us, "It is rather the other way about and it is the word which brings in the meaning which the image and its original conception lack."[19] Richards cautions against the mistaking of what he has been calling the tenor-vehicle antithesis for that between the metaphor (the double unit including 'tenor' and 'vehicle' and its meaning). It is easy to confuse these two antithesis especially when metaphor and its synonyms sometimes mean 'vehicle.'

Richards brings in the problem of Belief or doctrinal adhesions in poetry in the context of the command of metaphor. He points out that the error of mistaking the tenor-vehicle relation for the relation between tenor plus vehicle together and what they mean, has far-reaching consequences. The command of metaphor implies a command over the vital experience of life. Confusion about use of metaphor enters into the question of belief. If we read the *Divine Comedy* or *The Bible* aright, it is necessary for us to accept literally what it tells us. Richards cites in this context Eliot's remark about the *Divine Comedy* that the whole poem of Dante is one vast metaphor. It is a metaphor for the way of the soul from Inferno through Purgatoria to Paradiso. To Richards, as to F.R. Leavis, "literary criticism is concerned with more than literature. A serious interest in literature cannot be merely literary; indeed, not only must the seriousness involve, it is likely to derive from a perception of which must be a pre-occupation with the problem of social equity and order and of cultural health."[20] To Richards, the study of literature provides a methodology for the study of life. Hence, he affirms resolutely: "A command of metaphor, or a command of interpretation of metaphors, is command of life." Richards holds that "a command of metaphor or a command of interpretation can go deeper still into the pure control of the world that we make for ourselves to live in."[21]

The psycho-analysts have shown us with their discussions of transference how constantly modes of regarding, of living, of noting that have developed with one set of things or people, are shifted to another. The two concepts of 'transference' and 'resistance' were regarded by Freud as a direct expression of facts observed by him in the behaviour of his patients. Freud's conception of the discussions led by him to develop the concepts of 'transference' and 'projection.' In his *Psychopathology of Everyday Life*, Freud assembled hundreds of examples of lapses, errors and automations, all of which under his hands were made to reveal more or less hidden motives.[22] The psycho-analysts have shown us chiefly the pathology of these 'transferences.' Richards interprets these in terms of his theory of metaphor. He describes them as "cases say, tyrannism over the new situation, the tenor, and consequently because of this confusion of 'tenor' with 'vehicle.' The behaviour of the mental patient is inappropriate. The victim is unable to see the new person except in terms of the old passion and its accidents. He reads the situation only in terms of the figure, the archetypal image, the vehicle."[23] Richards proceeds to indicate that in healthy growth, tenor and vehicle—the new human relationship and the family constellation co-operate freely, and the resultant behaviour derives in due measure from both.

Thus, as Dr. K.R. Chatterjee points out, "Richards makes an extension of the literary instance of the use of metaphor to interpret problems of depth-psychology."[24] In this context, Richards once again refers to his faith in the development of psychology in the future to study the behaviour and meaning of words. "It is an old dream," he speculates, "that in time psychology might be able to tell us so much about our minds that we would at least become able to discover with some certainty what we mean by our words, and how we mean it. An opposite or complementary dream is that with enough improvement in Rhetoric, we may in time learn so much about words that they will tell us how our minds work."[25]

Having traced out 'tenor' and 'vehicle' as the essential ingredients of metaphor, Richards distinguishes between the poetic metaphor and other kinds. He concludes that the truly poetic metaphor is never merely decorative or logical or explanatory or illustrative. He claims that the transaction it sets up between 'tenor' and 'vehicle' results in a meaning to be clearly distinguishable from the 'tenor' which is not attainable without their interaction. He rightly claims that the vehicle is not normally mere embellishment of a tenor which is otherwise unchanged by it but vehicle and tenor in co-operation enrich the meaning of language transaction.

In *The Philosophy of Rhetoric*, Richards convincingly points out that imagery is not a single matter of calling attention to resemblances. As I have already pointed out, Richards draws attention to the "disparity element" in imagery, active as well as the resemblance element. Richards rendered a valuable service to criticism by demonstrating the rich and complex variety of the thought-relationships of which imagery is capable. One may insist with R.H. Fogle that while accepting and profiting by his remarks that the primary and determining factor of intelligible poetic imagery is likeness without it, no further relationship worth the name can exist at all. He rightly contends that the disparities between the two objects are of significance only when we have been impelled to bring them together by an anterior perception of these resemblances. Richards cites the metaphor of 'crawling' from *Hamlet* and *Gulliver's Travels*. In the example drawn from *Gulliver's Travels*, human beings are compared to small hateful vermin. This is a case of resemblance. But, in the Shakespearean example, the contrast with the Augustan positive conception of 'rational man' is implicit. It is true that the structure and the very existence of the image in both the cases depend upon the appropriateness of the idea of crawling to the idea of man. The Brobdingnagian king expresses his contempt for the nefarious activities of man by using the image of "crawling." The disparities operate only when the primary resemblance has been established. Richards's acute incisive analysis of the metaphoric or figurative use of language is to be commended.

Fogle, however, contends that "the conclusion to which professor Richards's examination of the problem of imagery (in his terms, metaphor) leads him is not useful in the critical analysis of poetry." He argues that "the ordering faculty which establishes the thought-relationship constitutive of imagery exists only in the mind of the reader, not in poetry itself."[26] Richards stresses the idea of the mind as a connecting organ and the freedom of the mind to fill in connection in all acts of interpretation. In *Seven Types of Ambiguity*, William Empson, Richards's brilliant disciple, speaks in a similar vein: "Statements are made as if they are connected and the reader is forced to consider their relations to himself."[27] Fogle marks the point that all Professor Richards's excellent criticism is marred by the subjectivist solipsistic tendency. Fogle lashes out the solipsistic tendency in Richards's excellent criticism: "A theory which places the burden of organizing poetic materials upon he readers instead of upon the poet is a slim basis for practical criticism."[28] We can say that actually Richards does not deny the existence of the poem as a linguistic artefact.

NOTES

1. I.A. Richards, *The Philosophy of Rhetoric* (OUP, New York, 1950), pp. 89-90.
2. *Ibid.*, p. 90.
3. I.A. Richards and C.K. Ogden, *The Meaning of Meaning*, p. 13.
4. I.A. Richards, *Principles of Literary Criticism*, p. 240.
5. I.A. Richards, *The Philosophy of Rhetoric*, p. 94.
6. *Ibid.*, p. 100.
7. *Ibid.*, p. 105.
8. *The Criterion*, Vol. XVII, No. 66, October, 1923, p. 127.
9. *Ibid.*
10. I.A. Richards, *The Philosophy of Rhetoric*, p. 129.
11. *Ibid.*, p. 133.
12. Herbert Reed ed. *Notes on Language and Style*, 1930, p. 18.
13. I.A. Richards, *The Philosophy of Rhetoric*, p. 133.
14. R.H. Fogle, *The Imagery of Shelley and Keats*, The University of North Candina Press, Chapel Hill, 1949, p. 10.
15. I.A. Richards, *The Philosophy of Rhetoric*, pp. 130-31.
16. *Ibid.*, p. 131.
17. *Ibid.*
18. Ezra Pound, A.*B.C. of Reading*, Faber, London, 1961, p. 36.
19. I.A. Richards, *The Philosophy of Rhetoric*, p. 131.
20. F.R. Leavis, *Introduction, Determinations*, 1934, Forcroft, The Forcroft Press, Inc, 1969, p. 2.
21. I.A. Richards, *The Philosophy of Rhetoric*, p. 135.
22. Robert S. Woodworth: *Contemporary School of Psychology*, (Methuen, London, 1942), p. 17.
23. I.A. Richards, *The Philosophy of Rhetoric*, p. 135.
24. K.R. Chaterjee, *I.A. Richards the Critic*: *The later Phase*, (Chaterjee Publication, Muzaffarpur, 1989), p. 68.
25. I.A. Richards, *The Philosophy of Rhetoric*, p. 68.
26. R.H. Fogle, *op. cit.*, p. 15.
27. William Empson, *Seven Types of Ambiguity*, p. 32.
28. R.H. Fogle, *op. cit.*, pp. 15-16.

Conception of Poetry in Richards's Later Writings

9

It is generally believed that from *Coleridge on Imagination* (1934) onwards, there is a radical shift in Richards's aesthetic thinking. It is argued that in his early writings, Richards assigned an inferior status to poetry by describing it as 'a pseudo-statement' in *Science and Poetry* (1926). This description is given in scientific terms. The business of the poet is to give order and coherence, and so freedom, to body of experience. The poet records his experience through his use of words. Richards points out that words work in the poem in two main fashions, as sensory stimuli and as symbols in the widest sense. The sensory aspect of the poem is not, in the least, independent of its ideational aspect, and for definite reasons it has prior importance in most poetry. Richards coined a special phrase 'pseudo-statements' to explain statements of the kind made in poetry. Cleanth Brooks and R.P. Warren have described poetry as a way of saying. Poetry is a kind of "saying." It is, however, a kind that many people, until they become well-acquainted with it, feel it rather peculiar and even useless. They feel this way for two reasons; the way of the saying and the "nature of the said." As for the way of the saying, the strongly marked rhythms, the frequent appearance of rhyme, and the figurative language may seem odd and distracting, and as for the "nature of the said," it generally contains neither a good, suspenseful story nor obviously useful information. Poetry, in short, may seem both unnatural and irrelevant.[1] Richards, in *Science and Poetry*, called such statements, as they occur in poetry, pseudo-statements. He tried to indicate thereby that they are not statements such as the statements which build up science or any fabric of factual discourse. Richards soon found out that his description of poetry as "pseudo-statement" annoyed critics. Richards calls literary pundits, as he sarcastically refers to the issue "The most powerful pundits prelates of the critical world joined in denouncing me for what? For saying as they alleged that such sentences are false statements and saying this in a peculiarly mean and underhand way."[2] Though Richards tried to explain the significance of his term "pseudo-statement," all his explanations failed to convince the literary pundits. It was thought that Richards was denigrating the status of poetry. His detractors were not convinced that he was not speaking of poetry in a pejorative sense. Critics were convinced that Richards was calling poetry names, treating it as much inferior to science.

In my opinion, this is an unfair and unjust indictment of such a passionate lover of poetry as Dr. Richards. Richards defends his position in *Speculative Instruments* in the spirit of self-appraisal. We must realize that corresponding to his theory of the two uses of language, which has been described in detail in an earlier chapter of this book, Richards has developed two angles of vision and two ways of looking at poetry. He quotes Blake as saying, "The eye, altering, alters all." As K.R. Chatterjee has pointed out in the preface to his book, *I.A. Richards The Critic: The Later Phase* (1989), "Richards's early books had been designed in terms of the scientific eye or the camera-eye. His later books, once again, show the alteration of his scientific eye into the emotive eye or Imaginative Perspective."[3] In his early writings on poetry, Richards adopts a Behaviouristic and Pragmatic view and so it appears that he accords an inferior status to poetry as a mode of knowledge as contrasted with scientific knowledge. Robert Wooster Stallman in his essay on "The New Critics" asserts: "The later Richards of *Coleridge on Imagination* (1934), however, has repudiated his former utilitarian theory of art."[4] Richards in *Coleridge on Imagination* thus defines poetry: "Poetry is the completest mode of utterance" This reveals Coleridge's famous description of the poet: "The poet, described in ideal perfection, brings the whole soul of man into activity, with the subordination of its faculties to each other, according to their relative worth and dignity."[5]

With *Coleridge on Imagination*, the later phase Richards has done a yeoman's service in renewing and extending the Coleridgean study of language and literature. As Kathleen Coburn has shrewdly noted, "Even before *Coleridge on Imagination* (1934), one could have predicted from the first two books, *The Meaning of Meaning* with C.K. Ogden (1923) and *Principles of Literary Criticism* (1924), in which Coleridge is referred to more often than any other critic, that some day Richards would write on Coleridge centrally."[6]

Coleridge was interested in the meaning and behaviour of words. The appeal of such myriad-minded person as Coleridge to Richards as the co-author of *The Meaning of Meaning* is quite obvious. In the words of Stanley Edgar Hyman, "the influence of Coleridge on Richards is a remarkable example of the meeting of minds across a century."[7] The impact of Coleridge's thought on Richards is pervasive, complicated and subtle. In the witty words of Hyman, "the development of Richards's books reads like the record of a love-affair."[8]

In the *Foundation of Aesthetics*, there is only a high-browish citation from Coleridge to pinpoint his mystical view of beauty. In *The Meaning of Meaning*, Coleridge figures only as the author of a rather high-flown statement about art. In *Principles of Literary Criticism*, after a number of mentions of Coleridge's poetry, Richards refers to the fourteenth chapter of *Biographia Literaria*. Richards describes *Biographia Literaria* as "that lumber –room of neglected wisdom which contains more hints towards a theory of poetry than all the rest ever written about the subject."[9] Richards picks up invaluable and luminous hints from *Biographia Literaria* particularly with reference to the concept of Imagination which he describes as Coleridge's greatest contribution to critical theory.[10] Richards is sharply opposed to the application of Transcendalist theories to the formulation of critical theory, but, setting this aside, there is enough in the description and in the many applications and considerations scattered through the *Biographia* and the *Lectures* to justify Coleridge's claim to have put his finger more nearly than anyone else upon the essential characteristic of poetic as of all valuable experience.[11]

Richards reminds us that one of Coleridge's clearest and most certain principles preserves the autonomy both of the poet and the critic. He cites with approval Coleridge's formulation: "Could a rule be given from without, poetry would cease to be poetry, and become a mechanical art." [12] Richards mentions with approval how Coleridge learnt form Bowyer, Head Master of the Grammar School, Christ's Hospital, that "Poetry, even of the loftiest and seemingly, that of the wildest odes, had a logic of its own, as severe as that of science, and more difficult because more subtle, more complex and dependent upon more and more figurative cases."[13] Richards is much influenced by Coleridge's studies in the severe inner logic of poetry. He learns from Coleridge the term "speculative instruments" to apply them to meditation on the creative or poetic process. Using Coleridge's words, Richards describes theories as "speculative instruments." Richards opposes T.S. Eliot's suggestion that "what was best in Coleridge's criticism came not from his philosophy so much as from his delicacy and subtlety of insight as he reflected upon his own experience of writing poetry."[14] Richards holds that Coleridge's insight into poetry could not be separated from the philosophic speculation. The speculation and the insight incessantly prompt one another. According to Richards, Coleridge's philosophy cannot be separated from his perception of poetry. Richards discovers that Coleridge's unique merit among English critics is the strenuous persistence with which he meditated philosophically upon criticism. His extra-ordinary gifts as a poet and as reader would not have produced what he has given us if he had not gone on, from his fourteenth year, thinking about poetry with an assiduity and enterprise that cannot be matched in the biography of another critic. Richards finds great significance in Coleridge's observation on *Venus and Adonis* that "the sense of musical delight with the power of producing it, is a gift of the imagination." "Coleridge," according to Richards, "took the psychology of the theory to a new level."[15]

Richards's theory of poetry is coloured by his perception of the Coleridgean distinction between Fancy and Imagination. In chapter XXXII of *Principles of Literary Criticism*, Richards as a semanticist lists at least six distinct senses of the word 'imagination.' He finds it convenient to separate them before passing on to consider the one, which is most important. First, Richards points out that the word 'imagination' means the production of vivid images, usually visual images. This is the commonest and the least interesting thing which is referred to by imagination. In the second sense, 'imagination' refers to the use of figurative language. "People who naturally employ metaphor and simile, especially when it is of an unusual kind, are said to have imagination."[16] This may or may not be accompanied by imagination in the other senses. In a narrower sense, third sense, imagination means "sympathetic reproducing of other people's states of mind, particularly their emotional states, is what is meant."[17] This kind of imagination is plainly a necessity for communication. Inventiveness, the bringing together of elements which are not ordinarily connected, is the fourth sense. In this sense of imagination, value is implied. In the fifth sense, we have that kind of relevant connection of things ordinarily thought of as disparate which is exemplified in scientific imagination. The faculty of imagination in this sense implied an ordering of experience in definite ways and for a definite end or purpose, not necessarily deliberate and conscious, but limited to a given field of phenomenon. Finally, Richards comes to the sense of imagination formulated in Coleridgean terms. In the words of Richards, "The original formulation was Coleridge's greatest contribution to critical theory, and except in the way of interpretation, it is hard to add anything to what he has said, though some things might be taken away from it with advantage."[18] Richards accepts the Coleridgean view of imagination after diverting it of its transcendental aspects. Richards cites with approval the following description of imagination:

"That synthetic and magical power, to which we have exclusively appropriated the name of imagination..... reveals itself in the balance or reconciliation of opposite or discordant qualities.... the sense of novelty and freshness, with old and familiar objects; a more than usual state of emotion, with more than usual order; judgement ever awake and steady self-possession with enthusiasm and feeling profound or vehement."

Further, Richards goes on to cite the following statement of Coleridge:

"The sense of musical delight.... with the power of reducing multitude into unity of effect, and modifying a series of thoughts by some one predominant thought or feeling" these are gifts of the imagination.[19]

Richards finds a valuable basis for his theory of poetry in Coleridge's separation of a primary from a secondary imagination. Richards finds in normal perception an equivalent for the primary imagination. Coleridge calls perception the primary imagination, it produces the usual world of the senses. The secondary imagination reforms this world, refines the normal routine act of perception and infuses it with poetry and every aspect of the routine world in which it is inverted with other values than those necessary for bare continuance as living beings. All the supernumerary perceptions which support civilized life are the product of the secondary imagination. Thus, there is a common source for poetry and other values of civilized life, and hence, there is a relation between them. In the light of Coleridge's separation between primary and the secondary imagination, Richards finds a connection between poetry and the ordering of life. Richards cites, with approval, Ben Jonson's view about the impossibilities of any man's, being a great poet without being first a good man at the same time. A great poet is a good man to the extent he is able to organize and order the heterogeneous experience forming his life. Richards, like Coleridge, finds both Primary and Secondary imagination vitally conducive to poetic activity in contrast to the mechanical power of Fancy, which merely collects and re-arranges, without making them, units of meaning already produced by the creative growing power of imagination. In the words of Richards, "In Imagination, the mind is growing; in Fancy, it is merely re-assembling products of its past creation, stereotyped as objects and obeying as such fixities and definites, the cases of Hartley's Association. The passage from the conception of the mind's doings as fancy, to that of the creative imagination is the passage from Hartley to Kant."[20]

Richards proceeds to give a psychological account of the two types of mental activity involved in Imagination and fancy. Coleridge often insisted that Fancy and Imagination are not exclusive of, or inimical to, one another; he believed in the co-presence of Fancy and Imagination. Imagination must include elements of Fancy. In fact, the higher intellectual powers can only act through a corresponding energy of the lower. Richards finds in Coleridge's doctrine of Fancy and Imagination a valuable method of comparison between experiences. With reference to Coleridge's example of a fanciful passage.

Fully gently now she takes him by the hand,
A lily prison'd in a goal of snow.
(*Venus and Adonis*; ll. 361-62)

Richards comments that here Shakespeare is making pleasing collections that are almost wholly unconnected with what he is writing about. Richards goes on to analyse Coleridge's instance of imagination describing Adonis' flight:

Look! How a bright star shooteth from the sky,
So glides he in the night from Venus's eye.

Richards perceptively notes that here the several units of meaning surrender almost all their local independence in a common co-operative purpose. At several places, Richards has translated Coleridge's ways of discussing Fancy and Imagination as suggesting mechanical treatment to Coleridge himself. Richards has given an interpretation of the transcendental Coleridgean theory from the viewpoint of a realist. Coleridge refers to the power by which one image or feeling is made to notify many others and by a sort of fusion to fuse many into one. Richards, like a realist philosopher, has modified Coleridge's theory of transcendental idealism. Richards in *Coleridge on Imagination*, uses phrases which suggest that it is the number of connection between the many, and the relation between these connections, that give the unity. Richards virtually re-formulates the celebrated Coleridgean doctrine. He discovers a unique merit in Coleridge's theory, for as descriptive devices the distinction between Fancy and Imagination point out actual differences in the experiences they apply to. With this, as Richards has noted, a fast step towards systematic comparisons between the structures of the meaning of poetry has been made and the way towards a further technique of comparison has been opened.

In seeking to re-formulate Coleridge's theory in modern psychological terms, Richards refers to the different kinds of meaning (Sense, Feeling, Intention and Tone, as in his *Practical Criticism*). According to Richards, imagination sets off a sort of effortless, exhilarating, continuing activity of the mind. This is a living process of the growth of meaning. In responding to an 'imagination' passage, we are invited to stretch our minds, and no one can flatter himself that he has ever finished the process of understanding and exhausting the full meaning of an imaginative passage. Richards is referring, in this context, to some whole, for it is in terms of a whole that the links of relevance between the units are relevant. To be able to blend into the whole, interanimating one another, the units, however, conceived, whether imaginative experiences, feelings or desires or attitudes, must be capable of dissolving, of being modified. In Fancy, on the other hand, the units do not fuse. They are separate concepts, such as these: 'A lily prison'd in a goal of snow' to give the sense of Venus's taking of Adonis's hand. The links between them are accidental, that is to say, there may be some links but they are here irrelevant, and merely distracting. John Crowe Ransom asserts that nobody is better entitled than Richards to the honours of being the discoverer of the importance of irrelevance in poetry. Indeed, for Richards, the distinguishing work of the imagination can be explained very much in terms of relevance.

The conception of imagination was used by Coleridge as a means of describing the wider and deeper powers of some poetry. Richards takes it as a descriptive psychological term in the sense that it points facts which explain certain poetic values. Under the checks of the senses and reason, of the activity of thought and the vivacity of the accumulated memory, the exercise of the Imagination is, for Coleridge, more valuable than the operations of Fancy. By relaxing those conditions, Richards seeks to make the terms purely descriptive.

Richards learns a valuable lesson from Coleridge's doctrine of Fancy and Imagination. On the basis of the distinction between Fancy and Imagination, Richards holds that we shall be able to discriminate between instances of Imagination which are valuable and which are not. This, in Richards's estimation, will lead to the formulation of a further theory. This will be a theory of value which will explain these differences of values. As Richards himself confesses, "This is the procedure I attempted to follow in *Principles of Literary Criticism.*"[21] We can distinguish between imaginative and fanciful poetry if we take account of the place and function of the imaginative and fanciful events in the whole activity of the mind and of this not only as an individual life but as a representation of what he calls the "all in each of human nature,"[22] the freedom which the individual shows with all men, provides the basis for the immediate intuitive feeling which enables him to respond to instances of imagination. This accounts for the Arnoldian dictum that great poetry interests the permanent passions.

Coleridge says that a poem contains the same elements as a prose-composition. The statement does not carry us far. We may take the element of a composition to be just the separable words or phrases into which a grammatical analysis could reduce it. But the meanings of words in poetry combine otherwise those in prose. Words are not necessarily the units of meaning. Richards reiterates his faith in the contextual theory of meaning. He refutes Herbert Read's statement that poetry may inhere in a single word. According to Richards, a word by itself, apart from an utterance, has no meaning. Richards carries out a multiple definition of "word" in the manner prescribed in *The Meaning of Meaning.* In the first sense, following Jeremy Bentham's *Theory of Fictions*, Richards defines words as "abstractive fictions, whose function is to collect for comparison, classes of their use. By the aid of these fictions, we describe innumerable words. (Speech acts as in sense 1) as examples of the same word (in sense 2).[23] We commonly take a part only of the meaning of a speech act as being the meaning of the word and count the rest of its meaning as our response to this meaning. In the third sense, by a word we may mean merely such and such sort of marks on paper, or heard sound, or movement of the speech organs which is the stimulus to an understanding of it. Fourthly, we treat a word as a sign containing within itself "a part or whole of the meaning."[24] We put its meaning into our working definition of word. The case of a poem provides a parallel case. The investment of words with meaning is an essential part of the right reading of poems. But there` are poems in which the limited dictionary meaning of words can sense the purpose of the understanding and enjoyment of the poem. Pope, at his best, as opposed to Keats at his best, serves as an example. In Pope's case, words are more or less taken as conventional signs. But in Keats's case, they are to be read as living inexhaustible meanings. As a rule, a part of the meaning is put into the word and the rest is left to be our response to the meaning. In terms of this analysis, the sense of a word have a wide range of variance. There is a vast scale of comprehensiveness. At one extreme words are taken as bare signs and at another extreme, words are taken as units into which some part or the whole of their meaning is projected.

According to Richards, good sense should be identified with the developed pose of choice, or in other words, with sanity. Coleridge's conception of good sense or taste or sanity is similar to Richards's idea of sincerity. Richards stresses the importance of formulating theories of literature. Good theories protect us from worse and the understanding of a good theory entails an exercise in careful and sometimes arduous thinking for persons with literary interests. Literary theory has its value. Richards deplores the tendency to disparage literary theories. Coleridge stated the problem of the place theory in life by a Platonic division between understanding (1) that is, theory and (2) Reason (that is, the entire operation of the mind). Judgment, whether of a passage of poetry or a politician, depends in the final analysis upon the reason or the entire operation of the mind which requires the whole man, the combination of practical and speculative intellect. The judgment that a passage is good is an act of "living," says Richards, for it involves the whole man.

Cleanth Brooks, in his review of *Coleridge on Imagination*, commends Richards for his brilliant defence of the validity of

Coleridge's famous distinction between the fancy and the imagination. "It is characteristic of his particular talent and method to light up such blind alleys of criticism. Here his interest in psychology serves him well."[25] Richards has done a great service to literary theory by showing what fusion in imagination means.

As Hotoph has noted, the idea of the fusion of unity as opposed to separateness, is applied by Richards in three further ways. First, he describes the fusion of the units of the poem with one another. Secondly, he emphasizes the function of perception with feeling of a word's sound with its meaning and of the reader's whole personality with the experience he is having. Richards describes the first fusion, that of perception with feeling, not in connection with art, but in connection with the way a person, say the world, or in Richards's idiom "Nature." As is characteristic of him, Richards carries out a multiple definition of "Nature" in which he distinguishes four senses. He does this in the context of his discussion of the two metaphysical doctrines, a "realist" and a "projective;" doctrines that can be found in Wordsworth's and Coleridge's poetry. 'Nature-I' is the influence to which the mind is subject. 'Nature-II' is the picture of the universe we project in response to I. 'Nature-I' is a selection of II which is perceived by all men alike the world of our practical everyday experience, whose laws are verified every minute of our lives. 'Nature-II' is a selection from III required by physicist to give an account of I. In the realist doctrine, man, through Nature, is linked with something other than himself which he perceives through her in the projective doctrine, he makes of her, as with a minor, a transformed image of his own being. Richards seeks to demonstrate how the realist and the projective doctrines are not really in conflict with one another. Richards reduces them to a fact of the mind which is their ground and origin. To concern ourself with a fact of the mind is to attend not only to "what is being said" by an utterance but also to "the saying of it." Thus, 'a fact of mind' includes 'what is being said.' It is a representation of a supposed sense of affairs but it includes also much more—'the history of the speaker's mind, and his feelings and attitudes in the moment of speaking with and conditions of their government in the future.[26] Reduced to a fact of the mind, both the realist and projective doctrines are true in their own way. Wordsworth and Coleridge have developed their doctrines through the use of the wind-harp image. Richards indicates that the wind-harp image symbolizes the language of poetry. The wind-harp image, Richards contends, can achieve the coalescence of the realist and the projective doctrines of the mind's intercourse with Nature. "It is the priviledge of poetry," Richards declares, "to preserve us from mistaking our notions either for things or for ourselves. Poetry is the completest mode of utterance."[27] This is really a singular statement of Dr. Richards who in *Science and Poetry* (1926) (later re-issued as *Poetries and Sciences* (1935) had asserted that much of poetry is concerned with making "pseudo-statements." The negation, pejorative implications of 'pseudo-statement' are completely dispelled in the definition of poetry as 'the completest mode of utterances....' Let us mark the use of the superlative degree of the adjective "complete." The implication is that if other forms of utterances such as the scientific, the referential, the dramatic, fictive forms of utterances, have their own completeness or adequacy, poetry surpasses all other forms of utterance in being the most complete (completest) or most adequate mode of saying. R.W. Stallman finds in this definition of poetry (given in *Coleridge on Imagination*) "a repudiation of Richards's former utilitarian theory of art."[28] We shall consider this problem at length in the next chapter. Meanwhile we recall that in *Science and Poetry*, Richards has stated that roughly and inadequately. Even in the dim light of present knowledge, we can say that words work in the poem in two main fashions—as sensory stimuli and, as in the widest sense, as symbols. The sensory side of the poem is not in the least independent of the other side, the symbolic aspect of the poem. For definite reasons, the sensory side of the poem has prior importance in most cases. Richards rightly contends that as poetry is a form of emotive utterance, the notion of 'truth' is distinguished from that as applied to a scientific statement. In a scientific or referential statement truth is ultimately a matter of verification as this is understood in the laboratory. In emotive utterance "truth" is primarily acceptability by some attitude. It is not the poet's business to make scientific statements, for the poet is not writing like a scientist. By describing poetry as 'the completest mode of utterance,' Richards refers to the integral vision of poetry as the expression of the whole soul of man in activity. Poetry is full of minor myths which are managed without the embarrassment or confusion with statements about matters of fact and without the uneasiness that comes from doubt as to their sanction. To Richards, as to Coleridge, the imagination actuated by the pure reason is the whole soul of man in activity.

Richards's conception of poetry in his later writings is tinctured by Coleridge's organic and integral view of poetry. Like Coleridge, Richards does not believe that higher poetry should have any conscious intention or purpose. Apart from some forms of applied poetry, some satires or some devotional poems, e.g. poetry, has no whither as opposed to the pleasures of an emotionally exciting journey. In a "just poem" as Coleridge points out, "the reader should be carried forward, not merely or chiefly by the mechanical impulse of curiosity or a restless desire to arrive at the final solution but by the pleasurable activity of mind excited by the attractions of the journey itself." Richards voices the concern of the free world at the use of art as a vehicle for propaganda in totalitarian states, and avers that the best poetry cannot be, and should not be, a vehicle of the propaganda. "With the best poetry, there is nowhere to arrive, no final solution. The poem is no ticket to the fortunate Isles, or even a Purgatory, or even to Moscow. The journey is its own end." Poetry exists for its own sake, though it is a vital sensuous embodiment of experience. Poem, which have a destination, or offer a final solution in the form of a supposed truth or suasion to a policy or the attainment of an end-state of consciousness or some temporary or permanent exclusive attitude to the world or society or to the self, have only a subordinate value. Instead of establishing, as the best poetry does, the norms of value, they have to be judged by the standards more inclusive than themselves.[29] Coleridge's account of imagination inevitably leads Richards to recognize that though every poem is a fabric of meaning, no pre-possessions that we can form can prescribe a structure for the meaning in poetry. Richards discovers that

Coleridge's theory of imagination offers an immense opportunity for improving our technique of understanding. Richards claims that Coleridge's theory of fancy and imagination was of revolutionary importance. With Coleridge we step across the threshold of a general theoretical study of language capable of opening to us new powers over our minds comparable to those which systematic physical inquiries are giving us over our environment. In the words of Richards, "the step across was of the same type as that which took Galileo into the modern world."[30] In Richards's opinion, Coleridge's theoretical equipment as a philosopher enriched his critical insight.

Coleridge on Imagination is mainly on poetry. It is Richards's last book mainly on poetry. *Principles of Literary Criticism* and its off-shoots, *Science and Poetry* and *Practical Criticism* are iconoclastic works with their heterodox ideas on poetry. *Coleridge on Imagination* marks the transition between Richards's late non-directionals such as *How to Read a Page*, *Speculative Instruments* and *So Much Nearer*. *Coleridge on Imagination* is important as a brilliant exposition of Coleridge's theory. "But it is still more important," says Cleanth Brooks, "as a further exposition of Richards's own position as a setforth in his earlier works."[31] Richards's formulation, this time, is in a form more concrete and more comprehensive, perhaps, because it is related to Coleridge's pronouncements. Richards relates Coleridge's concept of the imagination to his view that "poetry can save us." Richards holds that Coleridge is right in saying that it is the synthesizing power of the primary imagination that makes the world for us. The primary imagination is alike the act of normal perception; it gives us the usual world of the senses. It is this same power in the secondary aspect that the poet uses when he re-marks our world for us. The imagination in its secondary aspect give us not only poetry but the rest of the fabric of the world of our values. In Richards's view, poetry is capable of saving us by serving to give integration and meaning to a world that has been split up and dissected by the analytic power of science. Poetry should not be disparaged because it employs myths, for, according to Richards, science too employs myths, though those are myths with another purpose and another relevance. Richards discovers in the Coleridgean theory of imagination a theory of value, personality and learning. He vindicates the tremendous power of imagination by crowning it as a sovereign creative principle. In the words of R.P. Blackmur, "It is Richards's repeated declaration of faith in the poetic imagination as man's chief co-ordinating instrument that gives the book its passionate quality of importance."[32]

Irving Babbitt in his essay entitled "Coleridge On Imagination" had criticized Coleridge for his failure to follow the principles of Neo-Humanism. Ironically enough, Richards takes the title of his book from Babbitt's essay and demonstrates the modernity and originality of Coleridge's thought. Richards carefully analyses the scattered hints and remarks in Coleridge's various writings on the nature of imagination ranging from brief observations and perplexing adumbrations in letters and note-books to detailed discussions in "Biographia Literaria" and the statesman's Manual. Richards discovers that in Coleridge's organic system, the functioning of imagination is not restricted to the sphere of artistic creativity. Imagination operates in some form or other in all processes of human cognition and thought.

Richards's thoughts on the Art of Poetry in, The Philosophy of Rhetoric and Speculative Instruments:

We have already discussed Richards's developed theory of metaphor as it is formulated in "The Philosophy of Rhetoric." Richards believes in the paramount importance of the omnipresence of metaphor in the language of poetry. In terms of the context theory of meaning, Richards finds ambiguity to be an important part of language-transaction. While the old Rhetoric treated ambiguity as a fault or a blemish in language and hoped to confine or eliminate it, the new Rhetoric sees it as an indispensable means of most of our important utterances especially in poetry and religion. As in *The Meaning of Meaning* and *Science and Poetry*, Richards tends to equate poetry and religion in terms of their emotive use of language, our beliefs, feelings and attitudes tend to interfere with pure or neutral exposition. Statements imagery in poetry tend to have more than a single meaning in poetry tend to have more than a single meaning. Imagery in poetry is not a simple matter of calling attention to resemblances between apparently dissimilar objects. Richards shows that the disparity element is as active in imagery as in poetry as the resemblance element. Richards seeks to widen the meaning of metaphoric process in the language of poetry. Richards's later writings contain thought-provoking essays on the art of poetry. "The Interaction of Words" (1942) is a seminal essay on the language of poetry. As in *Coleridge on Imagination*, Richards tries to define "a word." Richards is now under the influence of Plato. The purposes of defining a word in poetics are different from those in psychology or linguistics. Richards is full of admiration for the marvellous and miraculous nature of language, which as an instrument of communication, works within us and for us. The nature of a word and its behaviour may be described as the very foundation, the source, the origin, the starting point and final cause of the intellectual life. To Richards, the definition of a word is one of the founding questions in the philosophy of poetry or like the dialectic study of poetry or like definitions of basic concepts in Mathematics and metaphysics. Richards revives for us the sense in which the poet is habitually described as a maker. The poet is the maker of beliefs in his own way. He makes himself and his world first, and thereby he proceeds to make other worlds and other men. According to Richards, the work or function of the poet is the maintenance and enlargement of the human spirit through remaking it under charging circumstances, through moulding and re-moulding the ever-varying flux. Richards describes these moulds as sets of words, interacting in manifold ways within a language. The mould-metaphor or images come from Plato. This is the dominant metaphor in Plato's educational philosophy. Plato gave the Greeks the idea of education, the idea of a university, an Academy. At first sight, the idea of a mould looks crude, for nothing could be less like mould than a word which endlessly changes its work in association with other words. The mould-metaphor in Platonic thought gives us a sense of surprise. It suggests the process of creation and the shaping power of imagination ever active in poetry. It points to the constant interaction and inter-animation of words in poetry. To Richards, "words are alive as our acts are alive though apart from the mind which uses them, they are nothing but agitations of the air or stains on paper."[33] The meanings of words grow as a cell grows with other cells. From this point of view, a word is permanent set of possibilities of understanding. To understand a word we should get to know the context of the other words with which it appears. We should understand the whole setting, present and past, in which it has developed as a part of our mind. Such things as pictures, music or the expressions of faces are other modes of language, other forms of expression, and these other modes of language can provide a parallel to the interaction of words. To quote Richards once again, "language, as understood, is the mind itself at work and these interactions of words are interdependencies of our own being." In Richards's poetic, there is a stress on the problem of interactions of words. A word is to be conceived as a component of an act of the mind. It is subtly dependent on the other components of this act and of other acts. Richards teaches us to study words together. No word in isolation has its proper meaning. "We understand no work except in and through its interactions with other words."[34]

To illustrate his thesis, Dr. Richards attempts a contrastive analysis of Donne's "First Anniversary" and Dryden's "Ode to the Pious Memory of the Accomplished Young Lady." A specimen of the metaphysical style of poetry is contrasted with a specimen of Restoration poetry. This gives Richards an opportunity of comparing two different types of interactions of words in poetry. In the Donne passage, Richards finds a prodigious activity between the words as we read them. Through the interaction and inter-animation of words, a new being is growing in the mind. In the Dryden passage, we have the poetry of statement; the words are in routine conventional relations "like peaceful diplomatic communications between nations." They do not induce revolutions in one another and are not thereby attempting to form a new order. Though Dryden's poem comes before our minds as a mature creation, we seem to create Donne's poem.[35] Dryden's is not a poetry in the technical sense of the word in which Donne's verses are, as Coleridge called them "wit's fire and fireblast" meaning's press and screw. The technique of metaphysical poetry consists in packing words with implications and increasing the interactions by making their implications explicit. This is the significant citation for Donne's and Dryden's use of metaphysical metaphor at its height.

In his essay entitled "The Resourcefulness of Words" (1940), included in *Speculative Instruments*, Richards pleads for a close attention to the language of poetry in terms of a systematic study of ambiguity. Richards states: "Words could not do their work unless they could rightly mean many more things than any one man in any one view can see them as meaning."[36] All non-technical words have ambiguity among the conditions of their service to us. Richards advises us that the best course for us is not to fear this ambiguity but to study and welcome it as an essential trait of the language of poetry. It is to be noted that Richards now drops the word 'ambiguity' with its confusing meaning and adopts the word 'resourcefulness' to describe the versality or the multiple meaning of words.

NOTES

1. Cleanth Brooks and Robert Penn Warren, *Understanding Poetry* (Holt, Rimehart and Winston, New York, 4th Edn. printed in Japan, 1985), p. 1.
2. I.A. Richards, *Speculative Instruments* (London, 1955), pp. 47-48.
3. K.R. Chatterjee, *I.A. Richards the Critic: The Later Phase* Muzaffarpur, (1989), Preface, p. 2.
4. R.W. Stallman ed: *Essays in Critiques and Criticism* (1920-1948) Ronald Press, New York, 1949), p. 494.
5. S.T. Coleridge, *Biographia Literaria* (Dent and sons, London, 1947), p. 151.
6. Reuben Brower et.al., ed., I.A. *Richards: Essays in His Honor*, New York, 1973, p. 238.
7. Stanley Edgar Hyman, *The Armed Vision* (New York, Alfred A. Knopf, 1952), p. 331.
8. *Ibid.*
9. I.A. Richards, *Principles of Literary Criticism*, p. 140.
10. *Ibid.*, p. 242.
11. *Ibid.*, p. 243.
12. S.T. Coleridge, *Biographia Literaria,* p. 190.
13. *Ibid.*, p. 3.

14. T.S. Eliot: *The Use of Poetry and the Use of Criticism* (Faber, London, 1933), p. 83.
15. I.A. Richards, *Coleridge on Imagination*, p. 10.
16. I.A. Richards, *Principles of Literary Criticism*, p. 239.
17. *Ibid.*
18. *Ibid.*, p. 242.
19. *Biographia Literaria*, p. 51.
20. I.A. Richards, *Coleridge on Imagination*, p. 59.
21. *Ibid.*, p. 96.
22. *Ibid.*, p. 97.
23. *Ibid.*, p. 104.
24. *Ibid.*, p. 106.
25. *The New Republic*, November 13, 1935, p. 26.
26. I.A. Richards, *Coleridge on Imagination*, p. 143.
27. *Ibid.*, p. 163.
28. R.W. Stallman ed. *Critiques and Essays in Criticism*, p. 494.
29. I.A. Richards, *Coleridge on Imagination*, p. 214.
30. *Ibid.*, p. 232.
31. *The New Republic*, November 13, 1935.
32. R.P. Blackmur, *The Nation*, April 10, 1936, p. 423.
33. Allen Tate ed. *The Language of Poetry*, Princeton University Press, p. 66.
34. *Ibid.*, p. 74.
35. *Ibid.*, p. 76.
36. I.A. Richards, *Speculative Instruments* (Routledge Kegan Paul, London, 1955), p. 74.

In Defence of I.A. Richards

10

Dr. Richards gave a new direction, a new dimension to the criticism of poetry which paved the way for New Criticism. Allen Tate describes Richards as "a master of laboratory technique,"[1] in his review of *Practical Criticism.* Tate's review has the significant heading "Poetry in the Laboratory." The heading points to the scientific orientation of Richards's study of poetry. Richards in his early writings investigates the nature of poetry in scientific terms. As Richards had been a student of Mental and Moral Philosophy at the university of Cambridge, his expert knowledge of psychology provided him with the tools of analysis. Reacting sharply against the metaphysical aesthetics, Richards commends scientific methods of analyzing aesthetic experiences and organization of words which constitute poetry. In his study of poetry, Richards follows the laboratory technique of scientific inquiry and investigation. He collects and analyses concrete, particular facts about responses to various types of poetry. He advocates empirical research into aesthetics.

Like a scientist, like a logician, Richards seeks to define the terms used in the vocabulary of literary criticism. Richards may be described as "a literary logician"[2] with a knowledge of psychology. He attempts a neat formal definition of a poem. According to Richards, the poem does not mean anything actual. Most usually by a poem we mean the artist's experience or the reader's apprehension of it. Richards has formulated a naturalistic theory of communication as opposed to the mystifying transcendental theory. Richards clearly states that we cannot get at the actual experience of the poet, but we receive something similar to it. There are divergent responses to poetry. Responses of the readers to the same poem differ. Hence, Richards refers to the standard experience of which the given poem is an expression. Richards defines a poem as a class of experiences which do not differ in any substantial form from a standard experience. This is a scientific definition in terms of its context.

Richards's conception of poetry is primarily based on his conception of the two functions or uses of language. Richards distinguishes between the descriptive or referential language of science and the expressive or emotive language of poetry. From this point of view, poetry is the supreme form of the emotive use of language. Richards identifies poetry as basically a linguistic activity. The poetic or emotive use of language is to be distinguished from the referential or cognitive value of language. Nobody should dispute this broad description of poetry in scientific terms.

But Richards's account of the poetic experience in *Principles of Literary Criticism* and *Science and Poetry* shows his tendency to explain the nature of the poetic experience. Like a behaviourist, in physio-psychological term, Richards discusses the impact of poetry on the nervous system. In the light of the developments in contemporary psychology, particularly behaviourism, Richards explains in detail how the mind works in the poetic experience. The stress on the stimulus-response theory of the mind as a clash of impulses, puzzles the common student of poetry. Richards's analysis of the impression of the printed words on the retina and his division of the response of the reader into the intellectual stream and the emotional stream may not be easily comprehensible to the common reader. There was an inevitable reaction against Richards's scientific study of poetry. Various charges have been levelled against Richards's account of poetry. It is alleged that his scientific treatment of the poetic process actually leads us away from the poem itself. Richards makes his psychological approach to poetry through states of mind whether of the poet or the reader or the listener or the speaker. It has been said that this may lead to solipsism. It means that the poem does not have any existence independently of the reader; for Richards seems to ignore the reality of the verbal structure erected by the poet. In *Scepticism and Poetry,* D.G. James alleges that Richards ignores the imaginative aspect of poetry. James dismisses *Principles of Literary Criticism* as the work for the most part of a psychologist.[3] A study of Richards's early books creates the impression. D.G. James argues that in poetry, which is the convergence by an imagination of the world, either in whole or in part, the details of psychological and physiological description in feelings, emotions and attitudes are at the expense of the recognition of the primary activity of the imagination. In D.G. James's hard-hitting words, "It is all Hamlet without the Prince."[4] He accuses Richards "of a signal dis-service to the advance of the theory of poetry."[5] James alleges that "Richards' love of poetry may be said to be of the cupboard variety; it is a means to an experience which is valuable for life."[6] Poetry, according to Richards, is a record of an organization of our impulses. The psychological analysis of the poetic experience is scientific. The mind is an organization of a system of impulses. No individual can live without a co-ordination of impulses. Poetry works on the nervous system. Good poetry, according to Richards, helps us to achieve a very perfect co-ordination of impulses.[7] To René Wellek, it appears that Richards tried to reduce poetry to a tonic for our nerves. Wellek concludes that Richards "failed when he tried to reduce poetry to a kind of tonic for our nerves, as he could not correctly describe the patterning of impulses supposedly achieved by poetry and could not relate the mysterious state of mind to any concrete work."[8] Montgomery Belgion in his critique *What is Criticism?* alleges that Richards misunderstood the aesthetic emotion and equated poetry with life.[9] Both F.R. Leavis and Allen Tate rejected Richards's theory of poetry and offered a trenchant criticism of his pseudo-scientific, pseudo-psychological and semasiological approach towards poetry. Richards is, thus, crticised for his misunderstanding and misinterpretation of the nature of poetry. Richards's psychological theory of value has been criticized for its mechanistic pseudo-scientific approach. Richards's value theory of the arts is based on utilitarian principles. Poetry is valuable because it helps us to systematically organize our impulses. Richards lays stress on the vague quantitative valuation of experience. Those experiences are said to be valuable which satisfy the large number of appetencies. Herbert Read is severely critical of such utilitarian theory of value. He objects to such a conception of value because in the end it reduces to a self-interest. He alleges that Richards ignores the existence of a moral consciousness.[10]

Richards's early writings reveal that though he takes much pains to describe the effect of reading poetry, he does not ignore the poem itself. While pinpointing a variety of our subjective responses to poems, Richards concentrates on the analysis of the meaning of words in poetry in terms of their interaction and inter-animation. His comments on individual poems in *Practical Criticism* clearly show that he is very much alive to the verbal structure erected by the poet. Hence, the charge of solipsism is contrary to facts. D.G. James' criticism of Richards sprouts from his failure to understand the significance of Richards's use of psychology to describe the effect of poetry on the nervous system; for any physical existence cannot ignore the impact of the contemplation of the fine arts on the nervous system. Richards's problem was to find a place for poetry in a world of fact. The materialistic view of life, which modern science has propounded, does not seem to leave any place for poetry and the fine arts in the conduct of life. As psychology impinges on the province of Richards, he like Herbert Read, is fully justified in borrowing from the science of psychology his vocabulary and tools of critical analysis.

Richards demonstrates that the study of good poetry is useful in terms of his theory of value derived from utilitarianism. Thus, we may infer that the purpose of Richards's theory of value is just to enable us to compare different experiences in respect of their value. Richards suggests that their value is a quantitative matter; confusion arises because as yet we do not know how to make the measurement required. It can be said in Richards's defence that the theory, in its own way, attempts to provide a system of measurement for the purpose in terms of the maximal satisfaction of appetencies. In fact, Richards's aesthetic is a magnificent corrective to the decadent aestheticism of the closing years of the last century. It may be seen as culmination of a reaction against Aestheticism or the doctrine of Art for Arts sake. Richards reacts against the decadent's move to isolate Art from life, aesthetic experiences from their rest of human activity. Richards demonstrates that art and the rest of human activity are continuous, not contrasting and that poetic experiences are valuable in the same way as any other experiences and they are to be judged by the same standards. Like Arnold, Richards has firm faith that poetry is capable of saving us. Richards champions the concept of art as survivor.

To my mind, it appears that most of these charges stem from a misunderstanding of Richards's scientific approach to the study of poetry. We must remember that Richards attempts a defence of poetry in this age of science and technology governed by computers. If we read Richards's last book *So Much Nearer* (1960), we find a satisfactory answer to most of the queries of the critics of Richards. It is wrong to say that Richards's love for poetry was of the cupboard variety. It is unfair to say that his love for poetry was fake. He had a deep love for poetry. This is confirmed by his extensive study of poetry when he was convalescing after an attack of tuberculosis in his youth.[11]

Richards's primary problem was to find a justification for poetry and the fine arts in an age dominated by the scientific, naturalistic, materialistic view of life. Before him, Aristotle, in ancient times, and Sir Philip Sidney and P.B. Shelley had attempted a defence of poetry. Plato banished poets from his *Republic* alleging that poets were liars. Aristotle in his *Poetics* defended poetry as a "more philosophical and higher thing than history." He stressed the therapeutic value of tragedy. Sidney defended poetry from the attacks of Puritans. Shelley exalted poetry as the highest expression of the creative imagination. Richards's problem is to find a place for poetry and the fine arts in a world of fact. In the present age of scientific analysis, we do not subscribe to the idealist and spiritual view of life which forms the basis for transcendental theories of art and literature. How can poetry be defended in this age of pragmatism, logical positivism and non-metaphysical philosophy? Richards attempts a pragmatic defence of poetry. He uses scientific methods and tools of scientific analysis to remove the scientist's objections to poetry. In *Science and Poetry*, he describes poetry as 'pseudo-statement' in order to distinguish the emotive language of poetry from the referential use of language in science. Statements in poetry are true in a way different from scientific statements. Poetic statements are true in the context of our emotional value. Psychology is a study of experience and of behaviour interpreted in terms of experience. As poetry deals with experience, a literary critic like Richards is justified in borrowing from the science of psychology the vocabulary and tools of statistical measurement and analysis. In his early writings, Richards used special psychological terminologies to describe his stipulated synthesis of conflicting impulses and tension in poetry. The psychological machinery makes Richards's study of poetry difficult. Cleanth Brooks observes: "The psychological machinery not only did not help; it actually got in his way and was worse than a distraction."[12] But Richards had to use scientific language to justify the value of poetry in the age of science. It was never his intention to reduce art to a set of scientific formulae just for the fun of it. He did not try to reduce poetry to a kind of tonic for our nerves; he simply tried to describe in psycho-physiological terms, the cathartic effect of reading good poetry. Aristotle's defence of tragic poetry is re-stated by Richards in psycho-physiological terms.

Richards is deeply influenced by Plato's ideas on education. In *So Much Nearer*, the teacher is advised to recall Plato's *Republic* and the aim of education to bring forth a new race of model human beings. Plato's thoughts on education are recorded by Richards in the form of metaphors from genetics or the science of breeding. Richards perceives that knowledge is essentially synoptic in character. Richards, in his study of the nature of poetry, tries to bring what he calls poetics and sciences into connection, in a comprehensive synoptic view of their relations with one another. Richards provides an instance from J.R. Oppenheimes' *The Age of Science* of the process of opposition and reconcilement between science and literature in the form of physics and poetry. Dirac, the eminent physicist, who worked on the quantum theory of radiation, scolded Oppenheimes, for the latter's habit of writing poetry as well as working at Physics.

Dirac did not understand how Oppenheimes could do both. How could he write poetry as well as work at physics? According to Dirac, in science, one tries to say something that no one knew before in a way that everyone can understand. Richards adds that in poetry one tries to say something which everyone knew before in a way which no one can understand.[13] In *So Much Nearer*, his last book, Richards passes beyond the frontiers of literary criticism to concentrate on problem of education. The study of literature, the study of poetry, is an essential part of education. Richards's switching over from literary criticism to education is perfectly natural. Coleridge, Arnold, Eliot and Leavis, all had become educators in the course of their career as literary critics. The results reported in *Practical Criticism* show that even most qualified students of English Literature showed gross failures to understand, to appreciate, or to judge poetry. Hence, Richards took upon himself the responsibility of studying poetry scientifically to show its utility.

Richards's essay on "The Future of Poetry" in *So Much Nearer* refers to early connections between poetry and prophecy. Richards cites with approval Shelley's eloquent defence of poets; that poets are the unacknowledged legislators of the world. Shelley makes a climactic claim for the authority of poets. Poets are eulogized as prophets. In this context, we are reminded of T.S. Eliot's warning to the critic "Honest criticism and sensitive appreciation is directed not upon the poet but upon the poetry."[14] This point is reiterated "To divert interest from the poet to the poetry is a laudable aim for it would conduce to a juster estimation of actual poetry, good and bad."[15] Richards proposes an amendation of the celebrated Shelleyan dictum. He seeks to amend the Shelleyan dictum with a view to heightening Shelley's claim for poetry. Richards agrees with Eliot's stress on poetry rather than on poets. He suggests that instead of saying "poets are the acknowledged legislators of the world," we should say that "Poems are the unacknowledged legislation of the world." A poet is, after all, a human being with limited powers and capacities and a limited span of life. Poetry (as a creation of art) is as immortal as the heart of man.

Richards believes with Arnold that "the future of poetry is immense."[16] Richards believes that poetry is as important to the survival of the human race as the material means of subsistence. Richards's defence of poetry is more inspiring and more stirring than Sidney's *Apology for Poetry* or Shelley's *A Defence of Poetry*. Richards does not believe in the phantom aesthetic state. For Richards, the experiences offered by poetry are not obtainable elsewhere. The function of poetry has not become obsolete with the phenomenal development of science and technology. Richards apprehends that the disappearance of poetry in modern industrial civilization will precipitate "a biological calamity of the first order."[17] Richards pleads for a return to the anonymity of the Homeric Poets or the ballad composers. He proposes a reversal of the Platonic ban of poetry as formulated in his *Republic*. "A wise and powerful state would establish machinery making it easy to publish poetry but impossible to be identified as its author."[18] Poetry is the highest form of the emotive use language can offer. Poetry gives shape and form to an experience. In Richards's words, "The process of writing a poem in many instances consists of cajoling an unembodied something into its incarnation."[19] The poetic experience seeks its verbal medium by finding the words for itself. The strength of a passage of poetry comes from the phonologic and morphologic network linking words with words (their rhyme field, root-branching and so on) and from the semantic network of substitutions, oppositions, implications and associations which by careless routes links every word with every other and from the mutual control of contexts.[20] The language of poetry is thus an instrument for the pursuit and control of meanings. Poetry, like fine arts, is a storehouse of recorded values. Richards points to the inseparability of form and content in poetry. Poetry is not simply the thing said, but the way of saying it. What is said in poetry, depends on how it is said and how it is said on what is said. Poetry is the completest mode of utterance. From the conception of poetry as pseudo-statement Richards has progressed to the conception of poetry as an organic whole, as the completest mode of utterance. What we say and how we say it, are inseparable in utterances which are complete. In whole utterances, rhythm, stress, intention, pausing, the expression of a face, gestures are as important as the choice of words. All these things moderate one another, qualify one another and adjust one another to the overall aim. The overall aim only finds itself through all these. According to Richards, no separation can be made between form and content, between message and signal in poetry. To express his idea more effectively, Richards quotes the following memorable lines from Yeats' 'Among school children'

"O body swayed to music, O brightening glance,
How can we know the dancer from the dance?"

The dancer cannot be separated from the dance, the poet cannot be separated from the poetry. Poetry exemplifies the interdependence, the unity of content and form, of sprit and letter, of intuition and expression.

Richards, thus, states the value of the record of the poetic experience. The study of best poetry promotes a healthy growth of the mind "it is our exemplar for that kind of mutual and just control of part by part which is health."[21]

NOTES

1. Allan Tate, *The New Republic*, December 18, 1929, p. 113.
2. I.A. Richards, *Principles of Literary Criticism*, p. 226.
3. D.G. James, *Scepticism and Poetry* (G. Allen and Unwin, London, 1937), p. 59.
4. *Ibid.*
5. *Ibid.*, p. 8.
6. *Ibid.*, p. 57.
7. I.A. Richards, *op. cit.*, p. 57.
8. René Wellek, *Concepts of Criticism*, New Haven, ed, London, 1969, p. 51.
9. *The Criterion*, X, (1930), pp. 118-19.
10. *The Criterion*, 3 April, 1925, p. 447.
11. Reuben Brower et.al. ed, *I.A. Richards: Essays in His Honor* (New York, OUP, 1973), p. 149.
12. *Ibid.*, p. 150.
13. I.A. Richards, *Speculative Instruments*, p. 110.
14. T.S. Eliot, *Selected Prose*, p. 26.

15. *Ibid.*, p. 30.
16. Matthew Arnold, *Essays in Criticism,* Second series, Macmillan, London.
17. I.A. Richards, *Principles of Literary Criticism,* p. 234.
18. I.A. Richards, *So Much Nearer*, p. 152.
19. *Ibid.*, p. 172.
20. *Ibid.*, pp. 170-71.
21. *Ibid.*, p. 174.

I.A. Richards and New Criticism

11

I.A. Richards was that Cambridge professor of criticism who turned literary criticism upside down in the 1930s. As Terry Eagleton has noted "A major link between Cambridge English and the American New Criticism was the work of the Cambridge critic I.A. Richards."[1] Eagleton contends that if Leavis sought to redeem criticism by carrying on the work of Matthew Arnold, Richards sought in his works to lend it a firm basis on the principles of psychology. Society is in crisis, Richards argues, because historical change and scientific discovery in particular, has outstripped and devalued the traditional mythologies by which men and women have lived. The delicate equipoise of the human psyche has therefore been dangerously disturbed; and since religion will no longer serve to retrim it, poetry must do the job instead. Poetry, Richards remarks, "is capable of saving us; it is a perfectly possible means of overcoming chaos."[2] Like Arnold, Richards advances literature as a conscious ideology for re-constructing social order, and does so in the socially disruptive, economically decaying, politically unstable years which followed the Great war.

Richards claims that though modern science is a model of true knowledge, it leaves something to be desired emotionally. Richards concedes that unless some pseudo answers are supplied to pseudo questions like what? And why? society is likely to fall apart. The role of poetry is to supply such pseudo answers. Poetry is an 'emotive' rather than a 'referential' language, a kind of 'pseudo-statement' which appears to describe the world but in fact simply organizes our feelings about it in satisfying ways.

The best poetry is that which organizes the maximum number of impulses with the minimum amount of conflict or frustration. Without such psychic therapy, standards of value are likely to collapse beneath the "more sinister potentialities of the cinema and the loud-speaker."[3] Richards's quantifying, behaviorist model of the mind was in fact part of the social problem to which he was proposing a solution. Whereas Leavis waged war on the technologico-Benthamites, Richards tried to beat them at their own game. Linking the utilitarian theory of value to an essentially aesthetic view of human experience, Richards offers poetry as a means of 'exquisitely reconciling' the anarchy of modern existence. "No Life," Richards remarks, "can be excellent in which the elementary response are disorganized and confused."[4] Organizing the lower classes will ensure the survival of the higher, finer ones.

The American New Criticism, which flourished from the late 1930s to the 1950s, was deeply marked by these doctrines. New Criticism is generally taken to encompass the work of Eliot, Richards and perhaps also Leavis and William Empson, as well as a number of leading American critics like John Crowe Ransom, W.K. Wimsatt, Cleanth Brooks, Allen Tate, Monroe Beardsley and R.P. Blackmur. Richards inspired the New Criticism and won the admiration of poets such as T.S. Eliot. Trained originally in psychology, Richards penetrated into a new level of hard-headed thinking to literary criticism, pushing through the effusive waffling of critics past. Richards's work dealt mainly with poetry and in short, his burning question is what makes a poem great. Certain elements of the works of I.A. Richards were essential to the development of the New Criticism movement.

The Meaning of Meaning, *Principles of Literary Criticism* and *Practical Criticism* are well-known works by Richards. One of the essential elements found in these works is Richards's concept that poetry is psychological and not cognitive. Richards also pays a great deal of attention to the use of language in poetry. His approach to poetry is a psychological one, i.e. he would invade our discussions by insisting that what we think of as knowledge is less indicative of the objective than it is to our own subjective emotions and desires. Essentially, poetry is all well and good, but it has no real connection to the world. Its purpose is psychological rather than cognitive.

Eliot and Richards are jointly associated as pioneers of the movement of New Criticism. Both of them were among the most influential critics of the twentieth century. The only difference between them was that Eliot was descriptive and Richards theoretical. The latter provided the verbal analysis of poetry. New criticism is usually used for the literary theory and criticism that began with the work of I.A. Richards and T.S. Eliot before the war in England and was continued by figures such as John Crowe Ransom, W.K. Wimsatt, Cleanth Brooks and Allen Tate in the United States during the forties, fifties and sixties. Although it developed quite independently of the Russian Formalist School Structuralist Theory, there are some fundamental affinities between the two movements. Both rejected positivistic literary scholarship and called for a renewed attention to literature and other kinds of writing; and tried to define these differences in theoretical terms; both gave a central role in their definitions to ideas of structure and interrelatedness, and treated the literary text as object essentially independent of its author and its historical context. The major critic of the period was Dr. I.A. Richards who, like the formalists dealt with literature directly stressing the need to focus our attention on the written text rather than on the paratextual areas like biographical and historical facts. Richards seems to encourage 'unhistorical' readings of poems. Richards was merely interested in reader's response to literature and on the evaluation of this response. His criticism took the direction of aesthetic psychological analysis. *Practical Criticism* records his experiments with his Cambridge students in which he distributed poems for analysis without so much as a hint to the poet's name or biography or any other extra-textual information. He wanted to record his student's response to text. The result of his student's response in *Practical Criticism* convinced Richards of the urgency to evolve a system aiming at rigorous training in reading of poetry and he himself proposed a number of initial measures. He began with locating the strands of meaning that a poetic language contained. As. M.S. Nagarajan contends, "with him, this method of interpretation (demonstrated in *Practical Criticism*) originated in England, later spread to the

U.S. and finally, has come to dominate academic criticism the world over. This anti-historical criticism became New Criticism."[5]

Richards recommended a 'close-reading paraphrase.' Close-reading, like *Practical Criticism* meant detailed analytic interpretation As Eagleton puts it: "To call for close reading, in fact, is to do more than insist on due attentiveness to the text. It inescapably suggests an attention to this rather than to something else; to the 'words on the page' rather than the contexts which produced and surround them." Eagleton goes on to say that close-reading "encouraged the illusion that any piece of language, 'literary' or not, can be adequately studied or even understood in isolation. It was the beginning of a 'reification' of the literary work, the treatment of it as an object in itself, which was to be triumphantly consummated in the American New Criticism."[6]

At the turn of the century there arose a group of critics in England and the USA, who set about putting the house of literary criticism in order. People's attitudes were changing and so were their life views. Standing on the threshold of the twentieth century English literature was poised for revolutionary changes. The most noteworthy movement in twentieth century criticism goes by the name of New Criticism. The twentieth century poets rebelled against both—the single voice of authority and the idea of fixity. The new emphasis that was given to criticism earned the title 'New' for it. More or less around the same period of time this movement grew in stature on both sides of the Atlantic in England and the United States. There seems to have been some discontent with the literary situation in both these countries, at the turn of the century. There had been phenomenal industrial growth; but literary art and criticism had not kept pace with this.

T.S. Eliot was a great influential figure behind New Criticism. His essay "Tradition and Individual Talent", written in 1919 was a building block for much Anglo-American criticism. In his essay Eliot argues that writers must have 'the historical sense', which can be seen as a sense of tradition. Tradition to Eliot is the presence of the past. It is not the knowledge of specific events in history, but rather an encompassing feeling of past literature, which inspires the writer to write originally and with the spirit of the past in mind. In this way, the writing is not repetitious and handed down from the immediate predecessors, but is new material written in the spirit of the past. Eliot says that whenever a new work is written it will be compared to the past and that the value of existing works will be readjusted to accommodate the new work: this is conformity between the old and the new. Therefore, a poet should be aware that they will be judged by the standards of the past and compared to works that are thought to be 'good.' Besides tradition, the other issues Eliot raises in *Traditional and the Individual Talent* is the likening of writing to *science* and the detachment from emotion that a writer must have while writing in order to achieve this scientific state. Basically in his writing, Eliot emphasized science, 'Objectivity,' 'impersonality,' and that the poem should be the object of analysis, not the poet. Eliot also claimed that the poem should contain the 'essence' of tradition based on the great works of the past. With the publication of T.S. Eliot's *The Sacred Wood* (1920) began a trend in criticism which came to be called *New Criticism.* As Nagarajan puts it, "The term was put into circulation by Joel E. Spingram, and all its major practioners have been either English or American. Spingram is an authoritative historian of Renaissance criticism. He explained the theories of Croce in a booklet called *The New Criticism* in 1911, and later, in 1941, the poet John Crowe Ransom, the founder of *Kenyon Review,* wrote a book reviewing the criticism of I.A. Richards, T.S. Eliot and Yvor Winters, rather disparagingly to which he gave the title *The New Criticism* (1941). This title has come to stay. In Ransom's book, there is an essay 'wanted: an Ontological Critic'; where he pleads for an establishment of an intellectual movement that deserves to be named New Criticism."[7] But by the time Ransom published his book in 1941, New Criticism had become an established school.

Eliot's essays in his *The Sacred Wood* clearly show that he was in favour of technical criticism as against glib moralism and impressionism. The American New Criticism was a reactionary movement in its contempt for historical criticism. The altogether changed tone and tenor in criticism can be noticed in the works of John Crowe Ransom, Allen Tate, R.P. Blackmur, Kenneth Burke, Yvor Winters; and later in Cleanth Brooks, Robert Penn Warren and William Wimsatt. Eliot's influence with his *Sacred Wood* (1920) and the influence of Richards's *Principles of Literary*

Criticism (1924) were also contributory factors to the development of New Criticism. On the English side, besides Richards, Empson and the scrutiny critics, Leavis, L.C. Knights, and Derek Traversi can be cited as those who preferred and practiced this criticism. What brought these critics together was the opposition to the system of academic literary scholarship that existed during their time. New Criticism had to fight hard against a hostile atmosphere that prevailed in academic institutions. As scholarship can only supply facts at the service of interpretation, Tate wanted not history but criticism to judge literature. New Criticism first started as a movement replacing the bio-critical and historical methods that dominated literary studies in the nineteenth and early twentieth centuries.

Very much like Richards, New Criticism takes a stand that the nature of literary language is different from the scientific or common language. Common language is denotative whereas scientific language does not call attention to itself, but points to the world outside. Form of literary language is inseparable from its content, and its meaning. What a text means, and how it means it are one and the same. The work, in which all elements contribute to create an invisible whole, has an ideal, organic unity. Nagarajan contends, "This unity is that by which a new critic value a literary work. The organic unity makes for the complexity of a work. The interpretation of a work, and its evaluation become one and the same for New Critics. By explaining its unity, they are also establishing its value. The complexity of a work is often the result of multiple and conflicting meanings. These meanings are produced by such devices as irony, paradox, ambiguity, tension, etc. If a work should achieve some order, all these devices should help resolve the conflicts, and tensions produced in the work."[8] The New Critics maintain that their interpretations are based entirely on the context and the language of the text. New Criticism insisted on focusing on the text. The concentration of the New Critics on the linguistic aspects of a poem has immensely benefited the study of poetry.

F.R. Leavis contends that New Critics focus strongly on "the words on the page." Leavis was a teacher of Cambridge University. His employment as an educator had a profound affect on his criticism. Many of the other New Critics lived in the

United States. For Leavis, living across the ocean in England gave him a different, if related perspective. F.R. Leavis was not entirely a New Critic, but his close analysis of the poem itself ("the words on the page") and his belief that a poem should be self-sustaining, make him important to New Criticism. Leavis's major influences include T.S. Eliot and Matthew Arnold and his major works include *The Common Pursuit*, *The Great Tradition*, *Revaluation* and *Education and the University*.

Leavis believed that there were great works of literature. He also defined ideas about what was poetry and what was not. He did not hesitate to dismiss many popular authors, like Tennyson and Browning as non-poetic. He believed that poetry should express something personal about the poet and the poet should be emotionally involved with the poem. Leavis also believed that the poet was an enlightened being. The New Critics want to know how the work speaks itself through figures of speech and symbols. New Critics are interested in how the parts of text relate to create harmony, order, tension, paradox, ambivalence and ambiguity. They are primarily concerned with the language (verbal meaning) and the organization (overall structure) of a text. New Critics, Like I.A. Richards, focused on poetry and not on fiction. It dealt with how a work can be read objectively and accurately by examining the structure and form. Therefore, New Critics conclude that there is one single or correct interpretation of a text. New Criticism is not concerned with external circumstances like the biography of the author, historical context, and effects on the reader have a minimum interest in the content of the text (message/ideas).

When in the 1920's the New Criticism first emerged in public it was limited to a small group of professors and students. In only two decades its principles, values and proceedings were to become so pervasive and so much embedded in the study of literature, that they were almost equated with the very nature and essence of critical art. In his essay "Wanted: An Ontological Critic" (1941), John Crowe Ransom announced that it was time to identify a powerful intellectual movement which deserved to be called "a new criticism." The New Critics felt it was time to do away with the traditional approaches which took into account extra-textual considerations and/or separated the form of the art object from its meaning, refusing to regard the work as an integrated art-form. Some of these concerns are similar to those of the Russian formalists, but between the two critical schools there are also important differences.

We can very well now say that from the outset of the New Critics' activity, their formalism never got an extreme, pure and hard nature, but was always infused with broader humanistic concerns and never severed all connections with what is outside the form of the literary text.

The New Critics were first the members of an informal group of literary discussion, around the poet-scholar John Crowe Ransom and his students Allen Tate, Robert Penn Warren, and Cleanth Brooks. Ransom was editing *The Fugitive*, a poetry magazine which published traditional-patterned verse, and championed a conservative ideology, later on to be defined as southern Agrarianism. In the 1930s other critics, such as T.S. Eliot, I.A. Richards, William Empson, R.P. Blackmur, René Wellek, W.K. Wimsatt, K. Burke, Yvor Winters, joined them. By 1955 the current had completely lost its innovative image and was regarded by many as a dying trend, but in fact, as William Cain has pointed out, the New Critical attitudes, value and emphasis became "so deeply ingrained in English studies," that they were felt to be, for many decades, "the natural and definitive conditions for criticism in general," and not "the legacy of a particular movement."[9]

The moderately revolutionary spirit of the New Criticism is not a pure product of the formalist twentieth century. Some of its roots lie in the aesthetics of Kant and Coleridge, which was based on a theory of imagination emphasizing the concepts of harmony and poetic wholeness. Kant, in his *Critique of Judgment* insisted that aesthetic pleasure is purely disinterested and it is indifferent to the real existence of the contemplated thing. The New Critics are also indebted to the paradoxical Kantian notion of "purposeless finality." In the same treatise Kant maintained that those things which we like and consider beautiful seem to have been meant for the satisfaction of our needs and desires, although there is no rational evidence that there has been a purposeful intelligence to have produced them.

Basil Willey asserts that Richards is not only a prominent Coleridgean but is himself, in many important senses, the Coleridge of our time; like Coleridge, he has taught us that there can be no criticism without considering fundamental conceptions, that we must watch our minds as well as use them, attending especially to what we are doing when we use words like 'word', 'meaning', etc; like Coleridge, he sees poetry as bringing the whole soul of man into activity at the same time imposing upon it a more than usual order, and like him, he teaches that to experience poetry fully is to enjoy the bliss of 'the rectified mind and the freed heart;' unlike Coleridge, he does not subordinate his critical and psychological insights to an overriding metaphysical and religious programme, but in his impassioned defence of life-values in a world gone cold and inanimate he has more than a little of the prophetic too.

Samuel Taylor Coleridge in his *Biographia Literaria* propounded the organic principle as the constitutive definition of the poem. "The whole is in every part, and every part can be found in the whole. The poem is that piece of composition characterized, unlike works of science, by the immediate purpose of pleasure and also by special metric and phonetic arrangements; it produces delight as a whole and this delight is compatible with the distinct gratification generated by each component part, which harmonizes with the other elements."[10] T.E. Hulme elucidated Coleridge's concept quite graphically in his *Speculations: Essays on Humanism and the Philosophy of Art*: unlike mechanical complexity, vital or organic is that kind of complexity "in which the parts cannot be said to be elements as each one is modified by the other's presence, and each one to a certain extent is the whole. The leg of a chair by itself is still a leg. My leg by itself wouldn't be."[11] The idea of organism had been first highlighted in Aristotle's *Poetics* but Aristotle had focused on plot, which acquired with him an almost immaterial, transcendental quality, and not on poetic language, not on figures and style.

In Coleridge's view, expounded in *Biographia Literaria,* a great poem is the product of both the primary and the secondary imagination. The secondary imagination "dissolves, scatters, in order to re-create"[12] the material of the primary imagination; it represents creation as against vision. 'Contextualism' is yet another important principle which the New Critics borrowed from Coleridge. Coleridge viewed the poem as a product of the form-creating man; it had an independent existence, within the organic system of mutual relationships among the terms that made up the context of the poem. Thus, the poem was regarded outside any and all non-poetic contexts. The early development of the New Criticism was mostly influenced by the theories of I.A. Richards, who took over and expanded Coleridge's contextualist thought, and T.S. Eliot. If the New Critics over looked the psychological component in the critical doctrine of the English critic I.A. Richards, they took over in various forms his distinction between the symbolic and the emotive language, as well as that one between statements (conveyed by science) and pseudo-statements (conveyed by poetry), which impresses not through the "truth" it contains, but through its structural coherence. Richards's emphasis on metaphor as a constituent element of language, and on the determining role of irony and tension in poetry was also extremely influential with the New Criticism. According to him, high poetry is characterized by a balanced poise—an equilibrium of opposite factors always in a state of tension; irony, for instance, brings them into the poem as contending, complementary impulses. When in 1930 Richards's disciple, William Empson, published *Seven Types of Ambiguity*, this study, which apparently established the essential formalist strategies, was taken as a model by American New Critics. Likewise, T.S. Eliot's "impersonal theory of poetry" as he himself called it in "Traditional and Individual Talent,"[13] had an important impact on the New Critical thought. The well-known New Critical concept of "fallacy," referring to the traditional critics' erroneous emphasis on what is creation and interpretation and not on the text as such, owes a great deal to Eliot's views. Eliot's persuasions affected the New Critics not only by reinforcing their formalistic tendencies but also as concerns their ideological affiliation, that is outside the limits of their formalism.

Although the New Criticism was not quite a homogeneous movement, the fundamentals of the formalist doctrine promoted by this school are not hard to elicit. A few questions the New Critics raised and discussed are what is the literary work as an art form? What is the relation between its structural components and its meaning? Can one speak about the contents as distinct from the form of the poem? What is the best method for interpretation of a text?

The New Critics were not concerned with the issue of literariness. The texts they were analysing were comparatively shorter poems and the approach employed by the New Critics was an exacting 'close–reading.' Attention was paid to 'what' the text says and 'how' it does it. In general, the New Critics favoured precision and tightness, a discourse that employs irony and ambiguity. A poem contains everything that is needed for its interpretation, and critics are at fault if they resort to arguments which take into account extraneous elements in their demonstration. Every word in the text is significant, not only through its denotative, but also through its connotative force. Like the Russian formalists, the New Critics emphasized the principle according to which form and content are inseparable. As Mark Schorer has put it, "Modern criticism has shown that to speak of content as such is not to speak of art at all, but of experience; and that it is only when we speak of the achieved content, the from, the work of art as a work of art, that we speak as critics. The difference between content, or experience, and achieved content, or art, is technique."[14] The meaning of literary text cannot exist, i.e. outside and without an artful arrangement of words.

The question that arises then is what should be excluded from criticism? As a 'prescriptive' (not only descriptive) critical movement, the school of Ransom, Tate, Brooks and others stood out through its famous catalogue of "fallacies" and "heresies." As early as 1937 in *The World's Body*, J.C. Ransom had compiled a list of exclusions, settings out from the idea that it is easier to assert what criticism is not. Apart from the works of historical scholarship and of Neo-Humanism which R.S. Crane, too, had put on the negative list, Ransom first excludes "Personal Registrations."[15] J.C. Ransom contends that criticism should be objective, should cite the nature of the object rather than its effect upon the subject. Ransom's dismissal of receptionist criticism was later on clearly and strongly systematized by W.K.

Wimsatt and M.C. Beardsley in the well-known essay "The Affective Fallacy" (1949).

The second exclusion from the field of criticism concerns the procedures of "synopsis and paraphrase." Even if they are used by genuine critic sometimes, he or she does not consider the plot as identical with the real content, but just as an abstract from it. This idea was later on expanded by Cleanth Brooks, in "The Heresy of Paraphrase" (the last chapter of his book *The Well Wrought Urn*, 1947) where he opposed the notion of "content" or "subject matter" to that of "structure" on which the value of literary work actually depends. It is heretical to summarize the content of a text, and thus to overlook its form.

Another item on Ransom's catalogue refers to what he calls "historical studies," in fact including historical, biographic, bibliographic ones as well as "comparative literature." Linguistic studies are also mentioned by Ransom on the negative list. In the end, ransom mentions any other studies which represent an abstract or prose content taken out of the work such as those dealing with Spenser's view of the Irish question, Shakespeare's understanding of the law, Milton's geography and so on.

To Ransom's catalogue of "uncritical" procedures we should also add "The Intentional Fallacy," as it was named in another essay by Wimsatt and Beardsley, bearing this title and published first in 1946. It refers to the critics' mistake of taking into account for their interpretation the "genesis" of the work, such as the author's biography, psychology and particularly his intentions. "It is only because an artifact works that we infer an intention of the artificer," the authors maintain. "'A poem should not mean but be.' A poem can be only through its meaning—since its medium is words—yet it is, simply is—in the sense that we have no excuse for inquiring what part is intended or meant."[16] If the value of a poem cannot be stated setting out from the author's intentions, or from the reader's reaction, if it does not depend on "content" or "subject matter" in the usual sense of these words, then in what terms can the critic approach it? Cleanth Brooks asserts that it is in terms of 'structure' that "the common goodness which the poems share will have to be stated."[17] Before Brooks, Ransom was also concerned with the nature of poetic structure, which he considered in opposition to that of science.

For Brooks "structure" is not quite a satisfactory term, as he acknowledges in *The Well Wrought Urn.* Transcending Ransom's use of the word, he means by it something far more internal than the metrical pattern or the sequence of images, far more complex than any statement abstracted for it. This concept of structure cannot be equated with "form," which is usually conceived as "a kind of envelop which 'contains' the content."[18] Poetic structure for Brooks means "a structure' of meanings, evaluations, and interpretations;" it is informed by a principle of unity, which seems to be one of "balancing and harmonizing connotations, attitudes, and meanings."[19] On the other hand, the principle of unity does not involve the arrangement of the elements in 'homogeneous' groupings, but it means uniting the like with the unlike. The process of structration necessarily involves moments of conflict, tension, contradictory attitudes. Therefore 'positive unity' is not achieved by an algebric simplification, but by a harmonization of the opposites within the poem.

According to Brooks, this accounts for the frequent occurance, in the New Critics' Lexicon of such terms designating conflict or divergence as "ambiguity," "paradox," "complex of attitudes" and "irony" the last one being the "most annoying to the reader."[20] The structure of the poem, according to Brooks, is like that of a play: it is based on conflict. Therefore, the conclusion of any literary text is the working out of the various tensions which result from propositions, metaphors, or symbols, and the final unity is the outcome of a process resembling the development of a drama. Commenting on the "personae," or the "speakers" in a poem, the New Critics emphasized the dramatic structure of the poem, based on an equilibrium of forces, be they rhetorical, symbolic, semantic and so on.

For Allen Tate the concept of 'tension' was the most useful formal tool at the critic's disposal, as "irony' and 'paradox' were for Brooks. The principle of tension sustains the whole structure of meaning, and as Tate declares in "Tension and Poetry" (1938), he derives it from lopping the prefixes off the logical terms 'extension' and 'intention.' The meaning of the poem is "the full organized body of all the extension and intension that we can find in it."[21] There is an infinite line between extreme extension and extreme intension and the readers select the meaning at the point they wish along that line, according to their personal drives, interests and approaches. Thus, the Platonist will tend to stay near the extension end, for he is more interested in deriving an abstraction of the object into a universal, and will try to find the shortest way with the "dissenting ambiguities" in the intensive part of the scale. For instance, Tate claims, the Platonist is likely to declare that Andrew Marvell's poem "To His Coy Mistress" is an invitation addressed to young men to behave immorally, and consequently he might want to censor it. Yet, this is only one side of the tension in the poem, for the rich intensive meaning, to which we should give equal weight, points to an essential phase of the human predicament, that is the conflict between sensuality and ascetism. In another illustration, Tate describes the metaphysical poet as beginning at or near the extensive end, and the romantic or symbolist one as beginning at the opposite point; however, each of them, "by a straining feat of the imagination tries to push his meanings as far as he can towards the opposite end, so as to occupy the entire scale."[22]

Within poetic structure, as seen by the New Critics, the concept of 'metaphor' acquired an almost theological status. Not only is it the essence of poetry, linking the concrete and historical with the abstract and universal elements in it, and differentiating poetry from scientific and ordinary language, but as Ransom states in "Poetry: A Note on Ontology" (1934), in any metaphorical assertion "there is a miraculism and a supernaturalism."[23]

In *Modern Poetry and the Tradition* (1939), Brooks emphasized the essentially functional character of all metaphor, which is best evinced in the Metaphysical Poet's verse. Their paradoxical conceits, in which intellectual and emotional qualities intermingle, contribute to achieve that "high seriousness" better than anything else. Metaphor is not only subsidiary, as the Romantic and neo-classical accounts suggest. It is not just the one alternative of the poets, but frequently the only means available to them. Brooks illustrates his view of metaphor with some verses from Andrew Marvell's poem "The Definition of Love": "As lines so loves oblique may well/Themselves in every Angle greet;/But ours so truly parallel;/Though infinite can never meet." In Brooks's words, "if we count as part of his statement, not only the proposition in its logical paraphrase, but the qualifications which it receives from the poet's emphasis and the poet's attitude—obviously the 'what' that is stated is stated by the metaphor, and only by the metaphor."[24]

Thus, with the New Criticism, as an echo of Coleridgean poetics, metaphor ceased to be a mere decorating device and became a means to insight, a way to discover truth. It is through metaphor that the mimetic and the cognitive values of literature intermingle, the wholeness of the poem rests upon other principles, which are essential for the ontology of the text: paradox, irony and ambiguity. Particularly the first two concepts are so often mentioned in connection with each other by Brooks and other New Critics, that, functionally and intrinsically, it seems that they tend to merge into a single complex rhetorical unit. Celebrated in turn as the essence of poetry, paradox and irony equally contribute to unifying the opposites in the poetic experience and to controlling the tensions within the poem from a rhetorical and semantic vantage point.

As a neo-critical term, 'Paradox' becomes prominent with the publication of Brooks's *The Well Wrought Urn* (1947): paradox springs "from the very nature of the poet's language," in which "connotations play as great a part as the denotations."[25] Otherwise, Brooks admits, few will agree that poetry is the language of paradox, because the latter defines the hard, bright and witty discourse of sophistry, not that of the soul, which is mainly emotive.

In Brooks's glossary, Irony has a very similar role to play in the poem. According to the precursor of the New Critics, I.A. Richards, irony is characteristic of poetry of the highest order, as it brings in the opposite, complementary impulses, in order to achieve a "balanced poise." When they talk about this poetic principle, Richards, Brooks and other New Critics do not primarily have in mind 'verbal irony' but the so-called 'situational irony'. Schlegel defined the latter type as a means of revealing through ambivalence, the paradoxical essence of the world. In *The Well Wrought Urn,* Brooks states that this kind of irony is the critics' most general term which points to that "recognition of incongruities" pervading all poetry and to the poet's controlled acceptance of them; it also points out to the "Kind of qualification which the various elements in a context receive from the context."[26] Celebrating dissension among the words and among the partial meanings of the literary work, the New Critics actually praise 'the organic wholeness' of the poem, as an essential prerequisite. This and the method of 'close-reading' have probably been the most powerful influences their school has exerted on the forthcoming generations of critics for about two decades."

René Wellek's essay "The New Criticism: Pro and Contra" weighs the New Criticism after the movement has grown out-of-date. Four charges are made against it. Wellek cites these charges. Its 'esoteric aestheticism' shows no concern with the social function of literature, and is like the revival of 'art for arts' sake movement. The New Critics are often called 'formalist' to expose their lack of social concerns. It is unhistorical, because it isolates a work from its origins, and context. It aims to make criticism 'scientific.' It is just a pedagogical tool like the French 'explication de texte,' useful only at the level of trying to learn to read literary texts, and poetry in particular.[27] Geoffrey Hartman in his essay, 'Beyond Formalism' powerfully expresses the hostility to New Criticism. The objection to New Criticism also came from other sources, before the final rejection came from the continental movements. The myth critics also attacked the New Critics. In his essay "The New Criticism: Pro and Contra," René Wellek observes, "The New Criticism has become a victim of the general attack on literature and art, of the 'deconstruction' of literary texts, of the new anarchy that allows a complete liberty of interpretation and even of self-confessed 'nihilism'."[28]

In defence of the New Critics it should be said that they were not averse to historical knowledge, they felt it should stand in subordination to the interpretation of the poem, it should serve as a means to another end. Many New Critics such as Brooks and Winters, are sound historical scholars. They have used history as a basic standard for judgment and interpretation. The role that the New Critics assign to criticism is good for poetry, and good even for society. For them, poetry is not cut off from the world, but is always directed to it and bound by it. The position that New Criticism occupies now in the area of literary studies is rather strange. For one thing it is not strictly speaking contemporary but the habit of reading it promoted during the

'40s through'60s is prevalent even now. Some important concepts it taught us are now absorbed in all the theories today. The 'close-reading' of texts that New Criticism taught us is now practised as a regular pedagogical method in teaching and learning. In this sense, New Criticism is never to be invalidated. However, their doctrine grew little by little out of fashion beginning with the late'50s, as the archetypal, psycho-analytical, and mainly structuralist approaches to literature were gaining ground. Of all these trends, structuralism was the only one possible to place in the same category of doctrines with the New Criticism, that is doctrines which imply the autonomous nature of the art of object. But apart from that, the cherished beliefs and goals of structuralism were so radically different that the two trends can hardly be viewed as relations.

One can find some convergence between the New Critical persuasions and some post structuralist views. It is no wonder that the deconstructive school has been described as a kind of New Criticism. Harold Bloom's interest in the poem as such, and his emphasis on the autonomy of literature, the deconstructors' belief that the surface of the text is only apparently quite, and their method of searching the text with a magnifying glass for relevant details can be mentioned in this respect; likewise, the post structuralist notion of the death of the author, or the idea that there is nothing outside the text. The deep motivations of these tenets put forward by the New Critics and respectively, by post structuralist authors are, however, as wide apart as can be.

New Criticism is a realization of the assumptions drawn from Aristotle, Kant and Coleridge, recreated and fused together, culminating in the modernist literary tradition. The New Criticism with its empiricism, exercised its influence on the institution of English studies for four decades, and still plays a significant role. One cannot deny the fact that only after the arrival of the New Critics, such other related disciplines as women's studies, Black studies, and comparative literature began to establish themselves. In this sense at least, New Criticism paved the way for widening the scope of discipline of English studies in various directions. "Of all critical doctrines that have prevailed on the English speaking scene in the post war decades, the New Criticism is perhaps the best qualified to be called a real school of critical approach to literature. Though it lacked the tightness and the scientific rigor of other formalistic currents, like the Russian school or the structuralist movement, though it was not the product of a single, circumscribed philosophical voice, and it was not spared the centrifugal moves of some dissident voices such as Yvor winters, Kenneth Burke and others, the New Criticism has the inner resources and the power to endure in the academic world for several decades. Today its closest (hostile) brother, the deconstructive school, is out of commission too, and cultural criticism has decisively taken the lead. Yet, even now, some of the New Critical procedures like close reading, the search for irony and paradox, are still there."

Though the once all-powerful, then all too vulnerable figure of New Criticism has been attacked from all sides by the structuralists, the deconstructionists, the new historicists, and the current multiplicity of socially-engaged criticism, it seems to persist in seeking a place in our contemporary scheme of things. New Criticism gave literature faculties a distinct subject—the literary work—and a teachable method for study. I.A. Richards's theory remains the living earth–the seed bed from which the seed of New Criticism sprouted and branched in several directions. The method of interpretation demonstrated in *Practical Criticism* by Richards has come to dominate academic criticism the world over. This anti-historical criticism became New Criticism which still influences many of the theories that try to leave it behind.

NOTES

1. Terry Eagleton, *Literary Theory: An Introduction,* second edn.(Maya Blackwell DOABA Publications, 2000), p. 38.
2. I.A. Richards, *Science and Poetry* (London, 1926), pp. 82-83.
3. I.A. Richards, *Principles of Literary Criticism* (London, 1963), p. 32.
4. *Ibid.*, p. 62.
5. M.S. Nagarajan, *English Literary Criticism and Theory* (Orient Longman Private Limited, India, 2006), p. 120.
6. Terry Eagleton, *Literary: Theory An Introduction,* second ed. (Maya Blackwell DOABA Publications 2000), p. 38.
7. M.S. Nagarajan, *English Literary Criticism and Theory* (Orient Longman Private Limited, India, 2006), p. 122.
8. *Ibid.*, pp. 125-26.

9. William E. Cain, *The Crisis in Criticism : Theory, Literature, and Reform in English Studies* (Baltimore: The John Hopkins University Press, 1984), p. 105.
10. S.T. Coleridge, *Biographia Literaria*, ed. J. Shawcross (London: Oxford University Press, 1907), Vol, II, pp. 10-11.
11. Thomas E. Hulme, *Speculations: Essays on Humanism and the Philosophy of Art* (London, Routledge and Kegan Paul, 1924), p. 139.
12. S.T. Coleridge, *Biographia Literaria*, Vol. I., p. 202.
13. T.S. Eliot, *Selected Essays* (London: Faber & Faber, 1932), p. 17.
14. Mark Schorer, "Technique as Discovery", *Hudson Review* I (Spring, 1948), p. 67.
15. John Crowe Ransom, 'Criticism Inc; *The World's Body* (New York: Scribner's 1938), p. 342.
16. W.K. Wimsatt. *The Verbal Icon*, p. 4.
17. Cleanth Brooks, *The Well Wrought Urn: Studies in the Structure of Poetry* (New York: Harcourt, Brace, 1947), p. 193.
18. *Ibid.*, p. 194.
19. *Ibid.*, p. 195.
20. *Ibid.*
21. Allen Tate, "Tension in Poetry," in *Collected Essays* (Denver: Allan Swallow, 1959), p. 82.
22. *Ibid.*
23. John Crowe Ransom, *The World's Body* (New York: Scribner's, 1938), p. 139.
24. Cleanth Brook's "Metaphor and the Tradition," in *Modern Poetry and the Tradition* (New York: Oxford University Press, 1965), p. 16.
25. Cleanth Brooks, *The Well Wrought Urn : Studies in the Structure of Poetry* (New York, Harcourt, Brace, 1947), p. 8.
26. *Ibid.*, p. 209.
27. René Wellek, "The New Criticism: Pro and Contra", *The Attack on Literature and Other Essays* (Chapel Hill: The North Corolina University Press, 1982), p. 87.
28. *Ibid.*, p. 102.

Bibliography

I. PRIMARY SOURCE: WORKS OF I.A. RICHARDS

A. Books written by I.A. Richards

The Foundation of Aesthetics (with C.K. Ogden and James Wood), London, George Allen and Unwin, 1922.

The Meaning of Meaning, A Study of the Influence of Language upon Thought and of the Science of Symbolism (with C.K. Ogden), London, Kegan Paul, 1923, Seventh ed. New York, 1945.

Principles of Literary Criticism, London, Kegan Paul, Trench, Trubner and Co. Ltd., New York, Harcourt, Brace, 1924, Eighth impression, 1945.

Poetries and Sciences, a re-issue of *Science and Poetry*; 1926, 1930. Routledge and Kegan Paul, London, First published 1926, 1970 edition.

Practical Criticism, London, Routledge and Kegan Paul, First published 1929.

Mencius on the Mind, London, Kegan Paul, 1932.

Basic Rules of Reason, London, Kegan Paul, 1933.

Coleridge on Imagination, New York, Harcourt Brace, 1935.

The Philosophy of Rhetoric, London, 1936, Oxford University Press, New York, 1950.

Interpretation in Teaching, London, Kegan Paul, 1938.

Speculative Instruments, Routledge and Kegan Paul, London, 1955.

So Much Nearer, Harcourt Brace, New York, 1968.

B. Articles by Richards

Emotive Language Still, *Yale Review*; 39 (1949), 109-18.

Emotive Meaning Again, *Speculative Instruments*; 39-56.

Gerald Hopkins, *New Verse*; No. I (January, 1933). 15-17.

Lawrence as a Poet, *New Verse*; No. I (January, 1933), 15-17.

The Interaction of Words, The Language of Poetry; *The Meseres Series in Literary Criticism*; ed. Allen Tate, Princeton University Press, 1942, 65-87.

The Practice of Interpretation, Reply by Richards to Montgomery Belgion, ('What is Criticism; *Criterion*, 10, October, 1930, 118-39) in *The Criterion*, 10, April, 1931, 410-20.

II. SECONDARY SOURCE: WRITINGS ON RICHARDS

A. Books Wholly on Richards

Brower, Reuben. et.al. ed. *I.A. Richards: Essays in His Honor*; Oxford University Press, New York, 1973.

Crane, Ronald S. Ed., *Critics and Criticism: Ancient and Modern*, Chacago, The University of Chicago Press, 1952.

Chatterjee, K.R., *I.A. Richards the Critic: The Later Phase*, Chatterjee Publication, Muzaffarpur, 1989.

——. *Understanding I.A. Richards's Principles of Literary Criticism*, Muzaffarpur, 1984.

Hotoph, W.H.A., *Language Thought and Comprehension*, University of Indiana Press, Bloomington, 1965.

Schiller, Jereme, P., *I.A. Richards Theory of Literature*, Yale University Press, New Haven, 1969.

B. Books Partially on Richards

Black, Max, *Language and Philosophy*, New York, 1949.

Gokak, V.K., *An Integral View of Poetry*, Abhinav Publications, New Delhi, London, 1961.

Henn, T.R., *The Harvest of Tragedy*, Methuen, London.

Hyman, Stanley Edgar, *The Armed Visions*, New York, Alfred A. Knopf, 1952.

James, D.G., *Scepticism and Poetry,* George Allen and Unwin, London, 1937.

Krieger, Murray, *The New Apologists for Poetry*, Minneapolis, University of Minnesota Press, 1956.

Ransom, John Crowe, *The New Criticism,* Norfolk, New Directions Press, 1942.

Rights, William, *Logic and Criticism*, Routledge and Kegan Paul, London, First Published, 1963, Second impression, 1965.

Stallman, Robert Winster ed.: *Critiques and Essays in Criticism*, 1920-1928, Ronald Press, New York, 1949.

Tate, Allen, *On the Limits of Poetry*, New York, Swallow Press and Win Morrow, 1948.

——, ed., *The Language of Poetry,* Princeton University Press, 1942.

Urban W.M., *Language and Reality,* George Allen and Unwin, London, 1951.

Watson, George, *The Literary Critics*, Penguin Books, 1962.

West, Allick, *Critics and Criticism,* London, Lawrence and Wishart, 1937.

Wellek, René, *Concepts of Criticism*, New Haven ed., London, 1969.

Wimsatt and Beardsley, *The Affective Fallacy or Critiques and Essays in Criticism*, 1920, 1948, New York, 1948.

Wimsatt, William K. Jr and Cleanth Brooks, *Literary Criticism: A Short History*, Alfred A Knopf, Inc., London, 1957, Reprinted, 1959.

C. Articles on Richards and Reviews

Bentley, Eric, "The Early I.A. Richards", *Rocky Mountain Review* 8 (winter, 1944), 29-36.

Belgion, Montgomery, "What is Criticism", *The Criterion,* X (1930), 118-39.

Blackmur, R.P., *The Nation*, April, 10, 1936, p. 423.

Brooks, Cleanth, "Review of *Coleridge on Imagination*", *The New Republic,* November, 13, 1935.

Empson, William, *The Criterion,* Vol. XVII, No. 66, October, 1923.

Pollock, T.C., "A Critique of I.A. Richards' Theory of Language and Literature", *A Theory of Meaning Analyzed*, Institute of General Semantics, Chicago, 1942, pp. 1-25.

Read, Herbert, "Review of *The Principles in The Criterion,* 3, April, 1925, 444-49.

Rickword, E., "Review of *Principles of Literary Criticism", Calendar of Modern Letters*; 1 April, 1925, 444-49.

Tate, Allen, "Review of *Practical Criticism* in 'Poetry in the laboratory'", *New Republic*, December, 18, 1929, 111-13.

Through Internet: "The New Criticism or Formalism with a New Face," 24 June 2007.

Schorer, Mark, "In Technique as Discovery", *Hudson Review,* I (Spring 1948) p. 67.

D. Other Books

Abrams, Meyer H., *The Mirror and the Lamp*, New York, Oxford University Press, 1953.

Arnold, Matthew, *Essays in Criticism* (second Series) London, Macmillan, 1960.

Baugh, Albert, C., *A History of the English Language,* New York, D. Appleton, Century Company, 1935.

——, *A Literary History of England*, New York, Appleton-Century-Crofts, 1948.

Bate, Walter J. ed., *Criticism, The Major Texts,* New York, Harcourt Brace and Co., 1948.

Bell, Clive, *Art,* Chatto & Windus, 1914, 1947, Stokes, 1914, 1924.

Bosanquet, Bernard, *A History of Aesthetics,* London, Swan, Sonnnenschein & Co., New York, Macmillan & Co., 1892.

Bodkin, Maud: *Archetypal Pattern in Poetry*, Oxford, 1934.

Brooks, Cleanth, Warren Robert Penn, *Understanding Poetry*, Holt, Rimehart and Winston, New York, 4th ed. Printed in Japan, 1985.

Brooks, Cleanth, *Modern Poetry and the Tradition*, Chapel Hill, 1939.

"Metaphor and the Tradition," *Modern Poetry and the Tradition* (New York, Oxford University Press, 1965).

——, *The Well Wrought Urn : Studies in the Structure of Poetry* (New York, Harcourt, Brace, 1947).

Brower, Reuben A., *The Fields of Light: An Experiment in Critical Reading,* New York, 1951.

Burke, Kenneth, "Four Master Tropes" (metaphor, metonymy, synecdoche and irony), *A Grammar of Motives*, New York, 1946, pp. 503-17.

Cain, William E., *The Crisis in Criticism: Theory, Literature, and Reform in English Studies* (Baltimore, The John Hopkins Press, 1984).

Caritt, E.F., *Philosophies of Beauty from Socrates to Robert Bridges,* Oxford University Press, 1931.

Caudwell, Christopher, *Illusion and Reality,* London, 1937.

Coleridge, S.T., *Biographia Literaria*, Dent and Sons, London, 1947.

——, *Biographia Literaria*, ed. J. Shawcross, (London, Oxford University Press, 1907), Vol. I, p. 202, Vol. II, pp. 10-11.

Crane, Ronald S., *The Language of Criticism and the Structure of Poetry*, Princeton, 1942.

Croce, Benedetto, *Aesthetics as Science of Expression and General Linguistic*, trans. Douglas Ainslie, 2nd edition, London, Macmillan & Co., 1922.

Daiches, David ed., *Critical Approaches to Literature*, Calcutta, Orient Longman, 1977.

Eliot, T.S., *The Use of Poetry and the Use of Criticism,* Faber, London, 1933. *Selected Prose*, London, 1932.

Elisio Vivas and Krieger Murray eds.: *The Problem of Aesthetics,* New York, 1953.

Empson, William, *Seven Types of Ambiguity*, London, 1930. (New ed., New York, 1948, Penguin Books, 1962).

Eagleton, Terry, *Literary Theory: An Introduction*, Second edition (Maya Blackwell, DOABA Publications, 2000).

Fogle, R.H., *The Imagery of Shelley and Keats*, The University of North Carolina Press, Chapel Hill, 1949.

Gardener, Helen, *On the Limits of Literary Criticism,* Oxford, 1957.

Hudson, Derek ed., *English Critical Essays*, Twentieth Century.

Hulme, Thomas E., *Speculations: Essays on Humanism and the Philosophy of Art* (London, Routledge & Kegan Paul, 1924).

Johnson, Samuel, *Lives of the Poets*, Macmillan, London, 1940.

Jung, Carl, *Modern Man in Search of Soul* (tr. Dell and Baynes), New York, 1934.

Lewis, Cecil Day, *The Poetic Image*, London, 1947.

Leavis, F.R., *Introduction, Determinations*, 1934, Forcroft, The Forcroft Press, Inc. 1969.

Mill, J.S., *Utilitarianism*, 1861.

Nagarajan, M.S., *English Literary Criticism and Theory* (Orient Longman Pvt. Ltd., India, 2006), pp. 120-22.

Osborne, Harold, *Aesthetic and Criticism,* London, 1955.

Passmore, John, *A Hundred Years of Philosophy,* Jerald Duckworth, London, 1957.

Pollock, Thomas C., *The Nature of Literature*, Princeton, 1942.

Pound Ezra, *The A.B.C. of Reading,* Faber and Faber, London, 1961.

Ransom, John Crowe, Criticism Inc. *The World's Body* (New York, Scribner's, 1938).

Read, Herbert, *Collected Essays in Literary Criticism,* Faber and Faber, London, 1938.

——, ed., *Notes on Language and Style*, 1930.

Saintsbury, George, *A History of Criticism and Literary Taste in Europe*, Vols. I, II, III, 4th ed. Edinburgh and London, William Blackwood & Sons, 1949.

Schelgel, *Lectures on Dramatic Art and Literature.*

Schorer, Mark et. al. ed. *Criticism, The Foundations of Modern Literary Judgment*, New York, Harcourt, Brace & Co., 1948.

Shipley, Joseph T., *Dictionary of World Literature: Criticism — Forms. Technique*, New York, The Philosophical Library, 1943.

——, *The Quest for Literature: A Survey of Literary Criticism*, Smith, 1931.

Smidt, Kristian, *Poetry and Belief in the Works of T.S. Eliot*, London, 1961.

Smith, James H. and Parks, Edd. W. eds.: *The Great Critics: An Anthology of Literary Criticism*, New York, W.W. Norton and Co.,1951.

Thompson, Denys, *Reading and Discrimination,* London, 1955.

Wasserstem William, ed., *A Dial Miscellany*, Syracuse University Press, 1963.

Wellek, René, *The Rise of English Literary History,* Chapel Hill, The University of North Carolina Press, 1941.

——, *A History of Modern Criticism, 1790-1950*, Vol. II, Yale, 1955.

——, "The New Criticism: Pro and Contra;" *The Attack on Literature and Other Essays* (Chapel Hill: The North Carolina University Press, 1982), p. 87.

Wellek, René and Warren, Austen, *Theory of Literature*, first published in U.S.A. 1949. Published in Great Britain by Jonathan Cape 1949, Second Edn. 1954: Third Edn. Published in Peregrine Books 1963, Reprinted 1966, 1969, 1970.

Wheelwright, Philip, *Metaphor and Reality*, Bloomington, Indiana, 1962.

Yeats, W.B., *Essays and Introduction*, Macmillan, London, 1961.